"A well and interestingly written book about a subject that needs this coverage. Don't ride the Rockies without it!"

— Eugene A. Sloane, author
Complete Book of All-Terrain Bicycles

"*Mountain Bike Adventures in the Northern Rockies* unveils adventure secrets in the region within the context of an environmentally sound philosophy."

— Pat Shea, Editor
Rocky Mountain Sports & Fitness

"We're excited about these volumes; they're just what the sport needs!"

— Bruce Feldman, Editor
Mountain Bike Magazine

"From the Black Hills to Idaho's panhandle, Mike McCoy's *Mountain Bike Adventures in the Northern Rockies* is the definitive guide to some of the country's best little-known, off-road bicycle routes."

—*Bicycling Magazine*

MOUNTAIN BIKE ADVENTURES IN

THE NORTHERN ROCKIES

Michael McCoy

The Mountaineers • Seattle

The Mountaineers: Organized 1906
" . . . to explore, study, preserve, and enjoy
the natural beauty of the Northwest."

Published by The Mountaineers
306 Second Avenue West, Seattle, Washington 98119

Published simultaneously in Canada by Douglas & McIntyre, Ltd.,
1615 Venables Street, Vancouver, B.C. V5L 2H1

3 2 1 0 9
5 4 3 2 1

Manufactured in the United States of America
Edited by Cathy Johnson
Maps by Carla Majernik
Cover photograph: Sawtooth Mountains; © David Stoecklein
All other photographs by the author
Cover design by Betty Watson
Book design by Nick Gregoric
Frontispiece: A scene along the Morrison Jeep Trail

Library of Congress Cataloging in Publication Data

McCoy, Michael, 1951-
    Mountain bike adventures in the Northern Rockies / Michael McCoy.
        p.   cm.
    Includes index.
    ISBN 0-89886-190-X
    1. Bicycle touring—West (U.S.)—Guide-books.   2. Bicycle touring—
Rocky Mountains—Guide-books.   3. All terrain bicycles.   4. West (U.S.)—
Description and travel—1981—Guide-books.   5. Rocky Mountains—Descrip-
tion and travel—Guide-books.   I. Mountaineers Title.
GV1045.5.W3M33   1988   89-3007
796.6'0978—dc19   CIP

Table of Contents

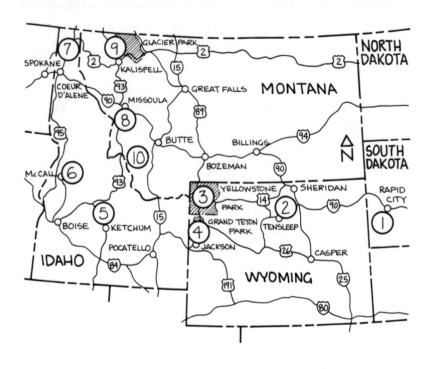

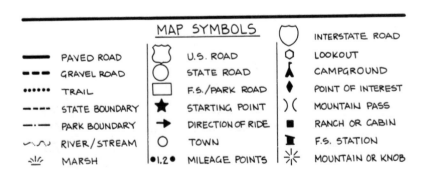

MAP SYMBOLS

——	PAVED ROAD	⬡ U.S. ROAD	⛨ INTERSTATE ROAD
---	GRAVEL ROAD	◯ STATE ROAD	⬡ LOOKOUT
••••••	TRAIL	▢ F.S./PARK ROAD	⛺ CAMPGROUND
----	STATE BOUNDARY	★ STARTING POINT	◆ POINT OF INTEREST
-·-·-	PARK BOUNDARY	→ DIRECTION OF RIDE	)(MOUNTAIN PASS
～～	RIVER/STREAM	◯ TOWN	■ RANCH OR CABIN
⋆	MARSH	•1.2• MILEAGE POINTS	⬛ F.S. STATION
			☀ MOUNTAIN OR KNOB

8

9

10

Preface

Nearly two decades ago, a friend let me try out his trailbike. I had often looked unfavorably upon people who rode their machines into the woods; why couldn't they hike and have just as much fun? Then they wouldn't bother other people and animals and tear up the trails.

Feeling somewhat guilty and sheepish, I discovered that I was having a "blast" on the motorcycle. But it still didn't feel right, although I was riding on a trail that was approved for use by trailbikes. My environmental sense was disturbed, and I didn't ride a motorbike in the woods again, until a job I had with the U.S. Forest Service mandated that I do so.

So, when I discovered mountain biking several years later, I took to it like a bird takes to the air. This new activity felt right. I found that it combined what I enjoyed most about hiking — solitude in the wilds — with the physical effort of road bicycling and the excitement I had experienced on the trailbike. Furthermore, it left behind what I felt to be the negative features of road cycling — the hassle and potential hazard of riding with cars and trucks — and the negative aspects of motorbiking — the obnoxious noise and fumes. I moved through the woods much faster than when I hiked, yet I could ride slowly right by deer and other animals without spooking them.

Yes, mountain biking felt right, but only in certain places. When I began reading about hiker vs. biker conflicts in such places as Point Reyes National Seashore, California, I thought to myself, "Uh-oh. Where is this going to end?"

That was a few years ago. Today there appears to be a growing number of mountain-bike riders who feel they're being cheated out of their rightful place on the trails in the national parks and federal wilderness areas. I believe mountain bikes should *not* be allowed on trails in these areas and have written this book hoping to demonstrate that there is no reason to even *consider* riding in them when scores of fantastic areas perfectly legal for mountain biking are going virtually untouched by fat tires. Unlike the widely known national parks and wilderness areas, many of these spots are cloaked in anonymity and receive few visitors beyond a scattering of local users. So, read, ride, and keep the rubber side down!

Acknowledgments

Numerous employees of government agencies provided valuable information and assistance when I was doing research for this guide. Especially helpful were Brian Vachowski of the Bighorn National Forest, Mark Van Every of the Bridger-Teton National Forest, Ramsey Bentley of the Pinedale (Wyoming) Resource District of the Bureau of Land Management, and Bruce Johnson and Joe Kipphut of the Missoula District of the Lolo National Forest.

Many private individuals provided general advice, specific route suggestions, and companionship. The biggest "thank-you" goes to my wife, Nancy McCullough-McCoy, who joined me on many of the featured rides. She suffered, among other things, a shoulder injury (from a fall off her bike) which finally required surgery to mend.

Thanks to map-maker Carla Majernik for her patience and steady hand, and to Cathy Johnson for her expertise in editing.

The staff and Editorial Review Committee at Mountaineers Books have exhibited foresight by recognizing the need for, and taking the lead in publishing, environmentally sound mountain-biking guides. They have my gratitude and respect.

This book is dedicated to my parents, Max and Mary McCoy.

Introduction

In recent years, mountain bikes and their cousins, "cruisers," have accounted for nearly 50 percent of all bicycles sold in the United States. In traveling around Yellowstone and Glacier national parks during the past few summers, I came to the realization that a large number of people — singles, couples, and families alike — are now mounting their fat-tire bikes atop their car roofs when they leave home on vacation. Yet, most of these people don't have a clear idea of how to go about finding the best rides. Oftentimes, they wind up pedaling along paved roads in the national parks, contending with the motorized hordes. Some end up disgruntled because they're not allowed to ride on the *trails* in the national parks — the same trails their bike-shop salesman back in Ohio or Texas may have misled them to believe their new bikes were designed for.

If only these folks knew that just outside the parks lie millions of acres of public lands administered by the states, the U.S. Forest Service (USFS), and the Bureau of Land Management (BLM) — lands ideally suited for mountain biking! The Northern Rockies — which are here defined as northern Wyoming, Montana, Idaho, and the western Dakotas — contain what is arguably the best and most varied mountain-biking opportunities of any section of North America. A century-plus of exploration, logging, and mining has left behind a legacy of trails, dirt roads, and jeep paths. From desert to dense forest to high mountain passes, it's all there, ready for the riding.

I have not attempted to create an all-inclusive atlas with this book. More potential mountain-biking routes exist in the Northern Rockies than any one person could ride in two lifetimes. This guide features 10 of the best areas I've found and details several day-rides for each.

Several of the chapters feature destinations which attract a lot of vacationers already, such as Sun Valley, Idaho and the country surrounding Glacier and Yellowstone national parks. Others pinpoint rides just outside some of the region's major cities, such as Missoula, Montana, and Rapid City, South Dakota. Some first-class mountain cycling is within minutes of these and other large communities. And others yet detail rides in areas where few people ever go, except on the way to somewhere else. The Big Hole Valley and the North Fork of the Flathead River are representative of this category.

Finally, Appendix A contains basic information on several other areas in the region that contain potentially top-notch mountain biking.

Mountain Bikes: Where To Ride Them

Because they're a means of "mechanical transport," mountain bikes are not permitted on the trails in national parks and federal wilderness areas. I consider them vehicles, just like trailbikes only not as noisy and not as potentially destructive to the terrain they traverse. For these reasons, the only *trail* riding featured in this guide is on trails specifically designated for off-road vehicles (ORVs) or specially recommended by the land administrators for mountain biking. Technically, most national forest trails *outside* wilderness areas are open to mountain bikes, even if they're not open to motorcycles. But I sense that more of them will become restricted as the number of mountain bikers continues to grow. Most trails in the Northern Rockies are unsuitable places to ride anyway because of the difficult terrain they traverse and because they're often used extensively by hikers and equestrians.

Some mountain-bike riders believe that bicycles are appropriate for travel in some of the wilderness areas. They maintain that bicycles do less damage to trails than do horses, which *are* allowed in the wilderness. They point out that skis are allowed in the wilderness areas, and aren't skis, they ask, a form of mechanical transport?

Perhaps they are, but these mountain bikers are skirting the real issue. Both horseback riders and skiers are traditional users of trails in the wilderness and were common on them long before the Wilderness Act of 1964. Permitting horseback riding in designated wilderness is perhaps not an ideal situation (I don't think anyone is seriously opposed to skiers in the wilderness), but we shouldn't fool ourselves into thinking that two wrongs make a right and allow new, inappropriate activities to take place in our wilderness areas. Permitting a new activity, such as mountain biking, would put a crack in the dam of wilderness protection. If the dam breaks, who knows what form of mechanical transport might then be found in the "wilderness" of the future — hang gliders? Pedal-powered flying machines (which already exist in prototypical form)?

Bob Marshall was one of the true heroes of the early wilderness movement in America. He knew what wilderness was, and I believe we should stick to his definition: "Regions which contain no permanent inhabitants, possess no means of mechanical conveyance, and are sufficiently spacious for a person to spend at least a week of active travel in them without crossing his own tracks." Mountain bikes cover too much ground too fast to be appropriate in protected wilderness areas.

There is a time and place for everything. I'm a conservationist and a nature lover. When I'm out on my bike in the woods, my senses are alive. I embrace the scent of pine and the sound of wind whistling through the

One of mountain biking's greatest appeals: being able to enjoy the scenery without worrying about traffic jams.

trees. But, I also like to go fast, especially on the downhills. I'm enjoying and appreciating nature, but at a much higher clip than when I'm hiking. Just as I would feel intruded upon if a truck came bouncing through the forest on one of my "private," closed-to-cars logging roads, hikers justifiably feel intruded upon when a mountain bike comes screaming down the trail at them. By cycling in the areas featured in this guide, you will ride guilt-free. Furthermore, you'll be in areas which are much less peopled than many of the popular hiking/horseback trails. This will help sidestep conflicts, resulting in a better situation for everyone.

I often find myself advising people to stop fretting over where they cannot — and should not — ride, and look around at all the places they can ride. The state of Idaho alone has 17,000 miles of trail; of these, 9500 are open to ORVs. With that many miles, you know that a lot of the trails are seeing very little use, so it's not as if we mountain bikers will be forced to contend with hordes of trailbikers. When you add in the thousands of miles of jeep trails and logging roads available for mountain biking, you begin to see that there's no reason to dwell on the off-limits areas. There is simply too much opportunity for first-class riding on the roads and trails which are legally and ethically open to mountain biking to waste time complaining about what's *not* open!

Finding Your Way
USING THIS GUIDE

The guide is divided into 10 chapters; each details one town or region. Appendix A features several additional places that offer good riding. Appendix B offers additional reading recommendations, Appendix C details map and information sources, and Appendix D lists suppliers of mail-order equipment.

The introduction to each chapter includes information about the area and where to get the necessary supplemental maps for the rides.

Each ride described is also shown on a map (in some cases, more than one ride appears on a single map). While it is possible to take the rides using only the maps in this guide, I strongly urge you to get the supplementary map listed for each trip. These maps will help you explore pathways not described — which I encourage you to do — or to find your way should you get off the route.

Three different categories of rides are included in the guide: point-to-point rides, out-and-back rides, and loops. Point to points are enjoyable because you actually go somewhere in accomplishing the ride. The obvious drawback: You either need to get a ride back to your point of origin or pedal back to the beginning. The out-and-backs in this book differ from point-to-points in that retracing your tracks is the only legal way to return to the point of origin. They are included only if they're very special, because most people don't like backtracking. Loops, of course, get you back to the starting point without backtracking.

For each individual ride, the following information is listed:
- General riding surface
- Beginning elevation
- Highest elevation
- Lowest elevation (if not the same as beginning elevation)
- Total distance of the ride
- Relative difficulty of the ride
- Time range to allow for the ride
- Best time of year for the ride
- Best time of week for the ride
- Supplemental maps needed

The difficulty ratings are subjective, based on how I felt after doing the rides, or how others with me reacted to them. As an example, a ride

In the fall in the Northern Rockies, you might find yourself riding in snow.

gaining 3000 well-graded feet of elevation might be rated as moderate, whereas one that gains 1000 feet could be rated as hard if those 1000 feet were extremely steep and demanded a fair amount of walking and pushing.

Regarding the "best time of week" recommendations: it's always best to check ahead; conditions may have changed since this book was written. You should definitely check with the U.S. Forest Service before planning a ride in an area which has active logging operations — you may discover that the chosen route is temporarily closed.

Some of the often-used abbreviations used in this book include USFS (U.S. Forest Service), NPS (National Park Service), BLM (Bureau of Land Management), ORV (off-road vehicle), and FR (forest road).

Keep in mind that this guide is not exhaustive. It contains about 40 mountain-bike day rides that are the "cream of the crop." There are many rides just as good waiting to be discovered. Appendix A will help you seek out some of these other great spots.

ODOMETERS

Mileages in the written narratives have been measured to the nearest tenth mile. Because variations in size and pressure of tires and in individual odometers can produce different measurements over identical ground, your mileage readings may not always be in exact agreement with those in this guide, but they will be close. It's also important to keep in mind that the exact mileage on a mountain-biking route is often not as relevant as the amount of up-and-down travel encountered. The combination of elevation gains and losses and the various riding surfaces makes it difficult to estimate the distance ridden.

Setting your bicycle up with an odometer is simply a necessity. There are several cyclo-computers available today that are easy to hook up; they range in price from reasonable to rather expensive. It isn't easy to estimate the distance ridden in a certain amount of time. As an experiment, I once kept my eyes off my odometer for an hour when riding in an area I hadn't previously explored. I guessed that I had ridden about 8 miles; the odometer registered 10.4! Having an instrument that closely measures the distance ridden eliminates the anxiety of losing track of how far you've gone. In an extreme situation, an odometer could become a lifesaver.

MAPS

Ordinarily, the best supplementary map is the USFS "Visitors Map" or "Travel Plan Map" for the area. Ordering information is at the end of each chapter introduction.

U.S. Geological Survey topographic maps ("topos") provide much information about the terrain, but the relatively small areas depicted make them impractical when covering large sections of ground quickly, as on a mountain bike. Topos are best for "reading the land" while moving slowly, as in hiking. Furthermore, they are often 10 or 20 years old and may not show current roads and four-wheel-drive tracks, which are of paramount importance to mountain bikers. All riders should at least be familiar with the use of topo maps and compass, and you *should* use topos when riding into areas not covered in this guide or where serious route-finding may be required. Some of the books listed in Appendix B are good resources for learning the basics.

ROAD AND TRAIL SIGNS

The signing of roads from one national forest to the next, and often within a single forest, tends to be inconsistent at best and absent at worst.

Several forests were in the middle of road renumbering during my visit, and numbers on USFS maps differed from those "on the ground." A further complication is that road signs may be defaced, stolen, or chewed up by porcupines. A sign that was brand-spanking new and looked like a permanent fixture when I visited the spot may now be unreadable or adorning someone's bedroom wall. Always keep this in mind, and if your odometer and/or map and/or common sense tell you that you're at a certain point, but you don't see the sign mentioned in the narrative — believe the first three and give up the sign as gone.

Gearing Up

YOUR BIKE

You may already have a mountain bike, but if not, several recently published books delve into this machine: how to choose one, how to maintain it, how to buy racks and packs, and so forth. Some of these books are listed in Appendix B. Regardless of your experience level, you'll learn a lot by picking up one of these books and reading it.

Mountain-biking is more demanding than paved-road riding, both on the body and on the bicycle. Mountain bikes are much hardier than their skinny-tired counterparts, but they need more maintenance. They get dirty a lot quicker than road bikes, and nuts and bolts get shaken loose more often. Wash your bike after a muddy ride and tighten any nut or bolt that even looks like it's thinking about coming loose. Be sure to check the bottom bracket and headset; these are notorious for coming loose on mountain bikes and could put you out of commission if they loosen in the woods and you don't have the tools to tighten them. Inspect the tires, check air pressure, lubricate your chain, and see if the brakes need adjustment before heading out on your next ride. Spin each wheel to make sure it's clearing the brake pads, and be sure the pads are contacting the rim and not the tire. At least once a year (preferably after the wet spring season), do a complete overhaul or have a trusted bike shop do it. Repack all bearings in fresh grease, change any frayed cables, get a new chain and freewheel if needed, and so on. If you're going to do the overhaul yourself, one of the books listed in Appendix B will lead you through the process relatively pain-free.

The single most effective way to reduce the chances of all sorts of problems, from flat tires to a sore neck, is to equip your bike with the proper rubber. To reduce import duties and to provide prospective showroom customers with a nimble test ride, manufacturers are putting 1.5-inch tires on many new mountain bikes. These tires are great for riding around town or touring on pavement; however, they're *too narrow* for all but the smoothest, driest conditions off-pavement. Narrow tires will cut into soft surfaces, creating difficult handling and excess trail or road damage. Compared to the fatter tires, they'll also flatten and give you rim dents more often, besides giving a rougher ride. There are many good tires being sold today; just make sure your bike is equipped with ones that fall in the 1.9-inch to 2.125-inch range.

The most common debilitating mechanical failure is the flat tire. Make sure your tires are always adequately inflated. If they're not, the tube may be pinched between the rim and a rock, resulting in a flat. Or, even worse, the rim can be severely dented. Also check your tires regularly for cuts, abrasions, and foreign objects.

Most good mountain bikes have enough bosses brazed onto the frame to accommodate at least two water-bottle carriers. When buying a bike, ask the dealer to throw in two carriers and two water bottles (many shops have bottles emblazoned with their logo, so you'll be advertising for them). If you already own a bike, be sure to add the carriers and

Some motorcycle trails are too rough or steep for mountain biking; others offer fine riding through splendid scenery.

bottles. Fill both bottles before heading out on even the shortest of rides.

Many mountain-bike riders use toe clips on their pedals. Although not a necessity, they do make pedaling more efficient, since you can gain power on the up-stroke as well as the down-stroke. They also hold feet in place on the rough stuff, resulting in fewer skinned shins. Strapless "mini-clips" are especially useful, as they are easier to get out of in bail-out situations, which tend to present themselves more often in mountain-biking than in road riding.

Another important item for the rough country is a quick-release adjuster for saddle height. Lowering the seat is a must for steep downhills and any situation when you may need to "dab" your foot on the ground to maintain balance.

While city riding may require only a pocket for your house keys, riding the backcountry requires extra equipment. Many excellent packs and racks are being made specifically for mountain bikes (see Appendix D for a listing of equipment suppliers). A rear rack alone will do for a short trip. However, the heavier loads for an extended trip require both rear and front racks, for mounting medium-capacity packs (between 1500 and 2000 cubic inches per pair). This arrangement makes for easier packing and a better-balanced bike. (For the front rack, stay away from "low riders," which are fine for road touring but have insufficient ground clearance for rough terrain.)

YOUR BODY

The best way to get in shape for mountain-biking is to ride your mountain bike in varying terrain. But most folks can't ride every day, nor should they try to; there's no better way to tire of something you really enjoy than to feel you must do it every day.

So, during the mountain-biking season, and during the one or two months preceding it (you folks who live where there is no winter can adjust this to your own likes), try to ride your bike two or three times per week. These rides can last as long as you want and they can be on- or off-pavement (or even off-ground on a wind-trainer or stationary bicycle). The riding days should be spread out as far as possible from one another, so that your body can rebuild after the minor damages inflicted upon it during a ride. Riding Tuesday, Thursday, and Saturday or Sunday gives maximum rest time between rides.

Exercise at least five days a week. On the days you don't bicycle, do some other form of exercising you enjoy. Anything — from badminton to basketball, from water aerobics to weight lifting — will help prevent the muscle imbalances that may surface if cycling is your only exercise.

Mountain-biking uses more of the upper body and torso than road cycling does, so exercise the upper body as well as the lower.

For optimum health and performance, be choosy about what "fuel" you put into your body. When you're out for a day ride, bring carbohydrates, and lots of them: fruit, gorp, bread, crackers, leftover pizza, and so forth. And, drink plenty of fluids. Appendix B will help you plan a nutritious, delicious diet.

CLOTHING

The most comfortable clothes for mountain-biking are those designed for the sport. However, there are a number of other clothing combinations that will work perfectly well, and probably save you some money. One good combination is running shorts (preferably with a polypropylene liner) and a cotton T-shirt (during warm, dry weather only — in the cold and wet, wear wool or polypropylene). Avoid pants or underwear with thick seams through the crotch; they will cause painful chafing, especially on long and/or rough rides.

As with clothing, mountain-biking shoes work well, but so do most lightweight, low-cut hiking boots. Whatever footwear you choose, make sure it is as appropriate for walking as it is for riding. In other words, leave the racing cleats at home!

To top off your outfit, always wear an ANSI (American National Standards Institute) — or Snell-approved hard-shell helmet, eye protection, and leather gloves.

Weather conditions, of course, may require extra clothing even for short rides. Some recommended foul-weather gear is listed in the Extended Overnight section.

TOOLS

Sooner or later you'll have to fix a flat, so always carry along the following tools:

- Frame-mounted pump
- 6-inch adjustable wrench (for removing wheel)
- 3 tire irons
- Patch kit
- Spare tube
- Slot and Phillips head screwdrivers
- Allen keys to fit your Allen bolts
- Spoke wrench
- 4 or 5 extra spokes
- Brake wrenches

- Chain lubricant
- One spare brake cable
- One spare derailleur cable
- Chain rivet remover
- Freewheel remover that fits your freewheel
- Pocket vise (works with freewheel remover)
- Small roll of electrical or duct tape
- Small pair of needle-nose pliers with cable cutter
- Different-sized nuts, bolts, and washers
- Small-to medium-sized hose clamps (for solving all kinds of problems, from loose racks to broken frames)
- Adjustable pliers
- 6-inch locking-grip pliers
- A few bearings packed in grease (in a film canister)

Many people would judge this list as excessive, for the chances of needing most of these items are quite slim, especially if you've determined before heading out that everything is tight, full of air, or otherwise in good condition. But each one can potentially prevent big problems, so decide for yourself. I've never used most of them in the field, but I pack them all along religiously. However, they won't do you much good unless you learn how to use them. It's not in the scope of this book to go into detail in mechanical matters, but these tools and their uses are well described in books listed in Appendix B.

OTHER ESSENTIALS

The mountain bike will get you much farther away from civilization in a given period of time than, for instance, hiking can. If, because of a breakdown or accident, you can't ride back out the 25 miles you just pedaled in, you could be in a lot of trouble. Twenty-five miles is a long walk, especially if you're pushing a bicycle! For this reason, there are some additional items you should always carry. This is a modified version of the "10 Essentials" that backpackers and skiers are advised to always carry:

- Waterproof matches or small butane lighter and fire-starter or candle
- Compass and map of the area
- Sharp pocket knife
- Water
- More than enough food for the time you plan to be out
- Spare clothing

- Flashlight or — better — battery-powered headlamp
- Plastic whistle
- High-quality sunglasses
- Space blanket for retaining body heat in an emergency

A first-aid kit should always be carried. Include the following:
- 2 triangular bandages or large bandanas
- Assortment of gauze patches and adhesive strips
- Moleskin for blisters
- Spenco 2nd skin for burns, blisters, "road rash"
- Adhesive tape
- Sunscreen (at least 15 SPF)
- Aspirin
- 3-inch elastic bandage
- Tweezers
- Baking soda for insect bites
- Insect repellent
- Antihistamine tablets for allergic reactions
- 2-inch gauze roll
- Antiseptic soap
- Needles and thread
- Single-edge razor blade
- Antibacterial ointment

All these first-aid materials should be carried in one small, water-proof container. Like tools, many of the items won't do any good if you don't know what they're for, or how to use them. It's your responsibility to yourself and your companions to be familiar with first-aid procedures. Read some of the books in the first-aid section of Appendix B or sign up for a course through your local Red Cross chapter.

Choose your campgrounds carefully.

Heading Out

RULES FOR OFF-PAVEMENT RIDERS

The National Off-Road Bicycle Association (NORBA) has generated a set of 11 rules known as the NORBA Code. This code should be followed by all mountain-bike riders:

1. I will yield the right of way to other non-motorized recreationists. I realize that people judge all cyclists by my actions.
2. I will slow down and use caution when approaching or overtaking another and will make my presence known well in advance.
3. I will maintain control of my speed at all times and will approach turns in anticipation of someone around the bend.
4. I will stay on designated trails to avoid trampling native vegetation and to minimize potential erosion to trails by not using muddy trails or short-cutting switchbacks.
5. I will not disturb wildlife or livestock.
6. I will not litter. I will pack out what I pack in, and pack out more than my share whenever possible.
7. I will respect public and private property, including trail use signs and no trespassing signs, and I will leave gates as I have found them.
8. I will always be self-sufficient, and my destination and travel speed will be determined by my ability, my equipment, the terrain, and the present and potential weather conditions.
9. I will not travel solo when bike-packing in remote areas. I will leave word of my destination and when I plan to return.
10. I will observe the practice of minimum impact bicycling by "taking only pictures and memories and leaving only waffle prints."
11. I will always wear a helmet when I ride.

One last point: Equestrians are common in the Northern Rockies, and sooner or later you will encounter them on a trail. Horses are skittish; approach them with care. A horse can spook and bolt at the snapping of a twig. If you come upon horseback riders — either from the front or rear — dismount and walk your bicycle. If possible, pass them on the low side of the trail, since horses are more frightened by objects above than below them. Talk to the horse or the rider as you pass, so that the horse knows you're human, and not some strange, two-wheeled life form.

It's also important to note that pack horses are generally more "spookable" than horses with riders. Don't let an encounter with you on a mountain bike result in a runaway packhorse!

RIDING TECHNIQUE

The best way to learn how to handle your mountain bike is by riding it. There are some basics, however, to keep in mind that will make the learning go more smoothly.

Going up. Learn to use your gears. To save your knees, always spin your pedals *at least* 75 complete revolutions per minute (racers, both on- and off-pavement, usually spin at 90+RPM). Try sitting down; try standing on the pedals, with your weight either forward over the handlebars or backward over the seat, depending on terrain. If you're in the lowest gear and the hill gets even steeper, move your weight still further back and push those pedals. If it gets too steep, dismount and walk before tipping over backward.

Going down. Learn how to brake, corner, lean and stay loose. Before my first mountain-bike ride, I'd been touring for years. I was smug; I figured I knew most of what there was to know — after all, how different could this mountain-biking really be? Before I headed down an incredibly steep pitch, my mentor warned me repeatedly not to overuse my front brake. But I did, and sure enough, I joined the O.T.B. (over-the-bars) Club. Luckily, I had my helmet on!

On downhills "feather" the brakes: Pump them gently to control speed. If you do need to make an all-out emergency stop, shift your weight back and apply the rear brake slightly more than the front (on the flats, however, apply both brakes equally). On extremely steep downhills, stand slightly, get your weight back over the rear tire, and squeeze the seat between your thighs for stability. On the steep, long downhills, lower the quick-release seat so you can sit lower on the bike.

When going around corners. Keep the inside pedal at the top of the revolution. Keeping the outside pedal down and with your weight on it serves two purposes: The inside pedal can't catch on the ground — preventing a possible wipe-out — and traction is improved. As you come into a sharp corner, first check your speed by sharply applying both brakes. Then, entering the turn, let up on the front brake and favor the rear one as you accelerate through the corner.

Read the coming terrain. Get in the habit of always looking 50 to 60 feet ahead. Then you're prepared to downshift, brake, or get up out of the saddle at the appropriate time. This will make your riding much more smooth and efficient. Look where you want to go, for you will naturally follow your line of sight.

A WORD ABOUT THE WEATHER

The weather in the Northern Rockies, as in most mountainous areas, is subject to rapid change and to extremes in temperature, wind, and precipitation. Take the equipment and tool lists seriously, and you'll be well prepared for whatever the weather deals out.

Also use common sense. Especially in the spring and fall, find out what the long-range forecast is before heading out on an extended trip. If the weather is forecast to turn out nasty, revise your plans accordingly.

Generally, the best months for riding in the Northern Rockies are July, August, and September. The lower elevation rides can be done in May and June, and perhaps April, but there's a good chance of getting wet while doing them. The higher roads and trails tend to be blocked by snow through May and, quite often, well into June. October can be a gorgeous month for riding in some years. Be very cautious before heading out on extended trips this late in the year, however.

STAYING HEALTHY

Health problems experienced in the mountains are usually a direct result of the weather and elevation, combined with a person's lack of preparedness for them.

Hypothermia, once called exposure, is a lowering of the body's core temperature, which can lead to collapse and death. It is the leading killer of outdoor recreationists. To avoid hypothermia, stay warm and *dry*. Dress (and undress) in layers, and try to maintain a point of equilibrium where you're neither cold nor sweating profusely — thereby wetting your clothes and becoming overly dehydrated as well. Wear a light "wicking" (non-absorbent) layer, such as polypropylene, directly against your skin, and drink more water than you think you need. Most cases of hypothermia occur at between 30° and 50° F, so it's a very real threat when cycling in the mountains, especially with the increased wind chill you experience riding at high speeds. Exhaustion compounds the problem, so get plenty of rest and don't go at it too hard.

Altitude sickness won't likely become severe at the elevations encountered on the rides described in this book. If you're not accustomed to them, however, elevations of 6000 to 10,000 feet can cause symptoms such as lack of appetite, nausea, and headaches. Acclimate gradually to these elevations, especially if you are coming from near sea level. Spend two or three days in the 5000- to 6000-foot range before heading to the higher elevations. To help limit the effects of high altitude, drink plenty of water, eat lots of energy-producing food, and don't push yourself too hard at first.

Sunburn, heat exhaustion, and heat stroke are concerns during the hot days of summer. Cover your entire body with lightweight clothes and/or sunscreen, and, once again, eat and drink often. If it becomes extremely hot, sit down for an hour or so in the shade and drink water.

OTHER POTENTIAL HAZARDS

Bears. Black bears are a potential concern in all of the areas featured in this guide, with the exception of the Black Hills (Chapter 1). In the Yellowstone (Chapter 3), Jackson Hole (Chapter 4), and North Fork (Chapter 9) locations, you'll be riding through grizzly habitat.

Although grizzlies are more aggressive than black bears, encounters with both species should be avoided. The chances that you'll run into bear problems while cycling are slim; there's more potential for conflicts when camping.

To bear-proof your camp, keep the site clean and store food and garbage properly — inside a car or a container provided for this purpose at the campground, if possible. If not, put the food and garbage in stuff sacks and hang from a branch no less than 10 feet above the ground and 4 feet from the tree trunk.

In bear country, NPS and USFS offices dispense detailed information on bears and how to avoid unexpected confrontations with them.

Lightning. Thundershowers and accompanying lightning storms are almost daily phenomena in the mountains during the hot days of summer. For this reason, if your route includes sections along ridgetops, try to finish that part of the ride early in the day. It's risky to ride along a ridgetop after noon or 1 p.m. in hot, thunderhead-forming weather.

If you do wind up on a ridgetop during a lightning storm, run, ride, or roll off of it as fast as you can! If you get caught in one of these slam-bammers, you'll discover the true meaning of fear. In addition to ridgetops, avoid lone trees, any open area, shallow caves, and the base or edge of cliffs. Safer locations include deep caves, heavily forested areas, and beneath and between big rocks in boulder fields. If you absolutely cannot get to safer ground, the USFS recommends that, in a treeless area, you sit on a small rock with insulating material (foam pad or a pack) under you, with only buttocks and feet touching the rock, and your hands clasped around your knees. If you are struck, the lightning bolt might not pass through your heart, due to the insulation.

Woodticks. From the first warm weather of spring until about mid-July, when the hot weather and low humidity force the adults to become

An exposed ridge like this is where you should not be riding during a thunderstorm.

inactive, woodticks are a concern. These eight-legged bloodsuckers can carry a number of diseases, including Rocky Mountain Spotted Fever and tick paralysis, both occasionally fatal (the most recent fatality in Montana, for instance, was in 1975, from Rocky Mountain Spotted Fever). Ticks also carry Lyme Disease. Recent research indicates that Lyme Disease may result in progressive deterioration of the nervous system, and that it has been widely mis-diagnosed as multiple sclerosis.

To avoid tick bites, when in grassy, brushy, or wooded areas, tuck your pant legs into your socks and tuck your shirt into your pants; wear light-colored clothing so you can spot the ticks; inspect yourself and your companions' backsides often; wear repellents, especially around shoes, socks, and cuffs; inspect your head and body well when you come in from a ride, since ticks seldom attach themselves during the first few hours (they crawl around looking for choice spots!).

If you *are* bitten by a tick, remove it as soon as you can. The suggested procedure is to grab the tick with small tweezers as near to your skin as possible, and gently pull it out. Be careful not to crush it, as its juices may contaminate the wound. Stick the miserable little creature in a jar in case health officials need it later for identification purposes. Treat the bite wound with an antiseptic and wash your hands thoroughly. If mouth parts are left in the wound, get medical help to have them removed. If, at any time during the two weeks after you were bitten, you develop a rash or flu-like symptoms, consult a doctor at once.

Bad water. Unfortunately, the days of safely sticking your cup in a mountain stream for a nice cold drink of water are about over. The one-celled animal known as *Giardia lamblia* is present in many cold, apparently pristine streams. Deposited in or near streams via animal droppings and human waste, the water-borne cyst is ingested when you drink from the stream. Upon entry into your body, the cyst attaches itself to your intestine wall. Body heat activates the cyst, and it enters its reproductive, or trophozoite stage. If you are susceptible to this bug, you'll get sick about two weeks later — often long enough after you drank the tainted water that you don't even think to blame the mountain stream for your ill health. The primary symptoms of giardiasis are severe diarrhea and nausea, which can last for months if not treated.

There are two effective, relatively simple ways to purify your water. You can heat it to boiling before drinking, or you can filter it through an approved filtration device; filtering is the more convenient method of purification, and it won't affect the taste of the water as boiling will.

To avoid adding to the problem of polluted waters, the "cat method" of human waste disposal, used by backpackers, is the best strategy. Carry some sort of digging tool (even a long knife blade will suffice). Select a spot that is at least 150 feet from the nearest water, and in the timber, if possible, avoiding damp, boggy areas. Dig a hole 6 to 8 inches across and deep and try to remove the sod in one piece (if sod exists). After use, burn your toilet paper (carry a butane lighter in your pocket for this and other uses), fill the hole with loose soil, and then tramp the sod in. Nature will take care of the rest.

Hunting season. For big game the hunting season varies from state to state. From September through November you'll find people shooting at animals in one or another of the Northern Rockies states. The woods aren't as dangerous during this period as some people might imagine, but it is a good idea to dress in bright colors — perhaps wear a blaze orange hunter's vest — and to make a little more noise than usual, just in case there's a hunter around the next bend. Often more people are out during the first few days of the season than later on.

Solo travel. Riding alone can be an enlightening experience. You'll see, hear, and smell more acutely than when you're with others. Because you're entirely dependent upon yourself and spoken words are not shattering the silence, your senses naturally become sharper, perhaps as a survival instinct.

But going solo also means you have to take full responsibility for your actions, and be doubly prepared for any emergency situation. *Always* tell a friend where you're going and when you plan to be back. If a search party has to be dispatched, the chances of finding you will be much

The clearest of mountain waters can hide Giardia lamblia, *the one-celled animal that causes giardiasis.*

greater if they know the general area you were riding in. Take the equipment lists very seriously if you are going to be riding alone, especially in the more remote areas. Think ahead and imagine yourself in various situations and prepare for them. Don't be caught asking yourself, "Oh, great — what do I do now?"

Fatigue. As in skiing and other activities which require good balance and sharp motor skills, mountain-biking accidents tend to occur when the rider is worn out. To avoid extreme fatigue, eat plenty of food and drink lots of water throughout the day, and treat yourself to frequent rest breaks. As you reach the end of a long day, avoid the temptation to ride fast over the sort of tricky sections you were able to accomplish earlier in the day, when you were fresh. Fatigue breeds sloppiness, and when tired you're much more likely to catch a pedal on a rock or slide a tire on loose gravel than when first starting out on a ride.

A NOTE ABOUT SAFETY

Bicycle travel, particularly in remote mountainous terrain, entails unavoidable risks that every traveler assumes and must be aware of and respect. The fact that a route or area is described in this book is not a representation that it will be safe for you. Rides vary in difficulty and in the amount of physical preparation and type of equipment needed to enjoy them safely. Some routes or their signing may have changed, or conditions on them may have deteriorated since this book was written. And, of course, conditions can change, even from day to day, owing to weather and other factors. A trip that is safe in good weather or for a highly conditioned, properly equipped mountain cyclist may not be safe at all under adverse weather conditions or for someone not properly conditioned or equipped.

You can minimize your risks by being knowledgeable, prepared, and alert. There is not space in this book for a general treatise on safety while traveling through remote areas, but a number of good books (see Appendix B: Recommended Reading) and public courses on the subject are available, and you should take advantage of them to increase your knowledge. Just as important, always be aware of your limitations and of existing conditions when you are cycling. If conditions are dangerous, or if you are not prepared to deal with the conditions safely, change your plans! It is better to have wasted a few days than to be the subject of a search and rescue or evacuation effort. These warnings are not intended to keep you from cycling in mountainous and remote areas. Many people enjoy safe cycling trips through such areas every year. However, one element of the beauty, freedom, and excitement of mountain bicycling is the presence of risks that do not confront us at home. When you cycle in the mountains, you assume those risks. They can be met safely, but only if you exercise your judgment and common sense.

THE EXTENDED OVERNIGHT

Aside from the special bicycle tools you'll want to carry, planning for an extended outing on a mountain bike is much the same as preparing for a backpacking trip. The list that follows includes items needed for mountain trips at high elevations. Judge for yourself what to leave home if, for example, you're going out only for an overnight and won't be encountering high elevations and/or unpredictable weather. Add to and subtract from this list as your experience grows. (A packing tip: Roll your clothes into "tubes," place them in clear plastic bags, and pack them vertically in your packs so the ends are visible.)

- Rainsuit/windsuit
- Long wool pants (for campwear)
- Polypropylene/Lycra-blend tights
- Warm sweater or polyester fleece jacket
- Lightweight wool sweater or wool shirt
- Wool or polypropylene mittens or gloves
- Wool or polypropylene stocking cap
- Spare lightweight shirts and underwear
- Athletic shoes (for campwear and stream crossings)
- Waterproof shoe covers
- Bathing suit
- Down- or synthetic-filled sleeping bag
- Sleeping pad
- Lightweight tent
- Backpacking stove, cook set and eating utensils
- More food than you'll need
- Toiletries: toothbrush, soap, etc.
- 3 or 4 elastic bungee cords

TRANSPORTING YOUR BIKE

Few of us are fortunate enough to be able to leave our houses and pedal directly into the hills, and even those who are will want to travel somewhere distant to ride now and then. So, unless you have a pickup truck that has an open bed into which you can toss your bike, you'll need to have a carrying rack.

There are many good, "high-tech" racks being sold today. Several of these have a major drawback: you need to take the bike's front wheel off and mount it onto the rack separately. Many mountain bikes are now equipped with quick-release wheels, but most older models don't have them.

If you'd rather not have to take the front wheel off at home, then put it back on at the trailhead, and repeat the entire process after the ride, use either a homemade rack utilizing two-by-fours and gutter brackets, or a manufactured rack on which the bicycles sit in troughs, with upright crossbars stabilizing the bikes laterally. Another good choice is the bumper "hanger" rack.

1

The Black Hills

The Black Hills lie predominantly within South Dakota, a state not generally recognized for its large mountain ranges; in fact, most outsiders' perception of South Dakota is something like a cross between Iowa and the Sahara Desert. But anyone who has spent time in the Black Hills knows that these are *mountains* not common hills (see if you consider them *hills* after riding the Cement Ridge Loop!). If only the Sioux word Pahasapa had been translated as "Black Mountains" rather than "Black Hills."

Unfortunately in this magical region the "tourist trap" has been honed to a fine art. Along the major roadways leading into the Black Hills, you begin to wonder how there is room left for anyone to live in the area, so numerous are the billboards advertising the overabundance of coming attractions. Perhaps Mount Rushmore, which represents the ultimate in man altering nature for his entertainment, has spawned this cancerous growth of roadside diversions.

The Wind Cave-Custer Loop leads through rolling, pine-studded prairie.

But behind the Reptile Gardens and the Bear Country USA's and beyond the Flintstones, the Wall Drugs, and the Trout Havens, lies country rich with streamside meadows, red-rock cliffs, forested hillsides, and granite spires. The Black Hills are laced with old roads and paths once used for logging, mining, and homesteading, providing the mountain biker with vast and varied biking opportunities.

Biologically, the Black Hills are a meeting ground of west and east. Several plant and bird species reach their farthest points east or west here. Ponderosa pine and pinon jays from the west co-exist with American elm and bluebirds from the east. Pine at the lower elevations, and pine mixed with white spruce higher up, dominate the slopes. Hardwoods such as oak, elm, ash, aspen, cottonwood, and birch are common along streams and are interspersed among coniferous stands.

Large mammals common to the Black Hills include white-tailed and mule deer, Rocky Mountain elk, and in the adjacent grasslands, pronghorn antelope. Audubon bighorn sheep, which were native to the Hills, became extinct near the turn of the century. The Rocky Mountain bighorn was introduced in 1959, and about 100 of them now inhabit Custer State Park.

Rocky Mountain goats were introduced in the 1920s. With their pure white coat and short, black horns, they can be seen around Harney Peak and the Needles. Another non-native critter is the burro, which once was used to haul tourists to the top of Harney Peak.

The mammal that is potentially of greatest concern to the mountain biker — at least on the Wind Cave–Custer Loop — is the American bison. There's a good chance you'll come across single individuals or even entire herds along the roads in Wind Cave National Park and Custer State Park. The rangers advise that you keep your distance — 100 yards at least — and wait for them to move on, which they will do sooner or later.

Some tips on bison body language could come in handy. If an animal's tail is raised, his head is wagging, or he is pawing the earth, be wary. If he is doing all three of these things, then, by all means, stand back! These are big, strong, and wild animals that don't take to being herded by bicyclists, and, they can run at 30 to 35 miles per hour. Be particularly cautious around cows when they are tending young calves and around bulls during the rut, which is ordinarily from August through early September in the Black Hills.

The Black Hills rise 3000 to 4000 feet above the plains below, with the highest point being Harney Peak, at 7242 feet. The Hills are about 120 miles long north to south, and 50 miles wide. They are somewhat like a layer cake which someone has sliced unevenly, exposing the various components. The Central Area, about 50 by 20 miles, is where the oldest rock in the range — some over 2 billion years old — is exposed. The Central Area contains distinctive, highly eroded spires and pinnacles, which you'll see north of the town of Custer. Some of these granites contain the precious minerals which made history in the Black Hills (and which are still making history — the Homestake Mine in the town of Lead yields more gold today than any other mine in America).

The Limestone Plateau encircles the Central Area. The plateau is characterized by high cliffs reaching above the valley floors. You'll see these in your travels through Spearfish and Little Spearfish canyons. Outside the plateau, in buried limestones, the caves common to the Black Hills are found.

Often termed the "racetrack," the Red Valley surrounds the Black Hills, lying outside of the sloping Limestone Plateau. Averaging 2 miles in width, this is an unforested area, the soils of which can become very mucky when wet. You'll see its characteristic red sandstone and siltstone on the Hell Canyon Loop ride.

Finally, forming the outside rim of the Hills is the Hogback Ridge. The outer slopes of the rim merge into the surrounding plains, and the inside slopes face the Red Valley. This ridge extends nearly unbroken around the Hills, with gaps found only where streams exit onto the plains. Petrified wood is common along the top of the ridge.

At the northern end of the Hills are several laccoliths, features formed by volcanic intrusion into the surrounding, older rock. Terry Peak, at 7071 feet, just southwest of the town of Lead, is the highest of these. Over in Wyoming, Devils Tower — the focus of our first national monument — is another such intrusion.

Because of the moderate elevations found in the Black Hills, they are a particularly good place to become acclimated to higher elevations before riding in the *really* high places farther to the west, such as the Bighorn Mountains and Jackson Hole, Wyoming. The roads in the Black Hills tend to keep going, "over the next knob" and into the adjacent drainage, in contrast to larger ranges, where many roads dead-end once they get into the precipitous, high basins. Especially if you're traveling into the region from points east, do some riding in the Black Hills. You'll find that this is no "second choice" mountain range. Rather, these mountains offer some of the most enjoyable and varied riding conditions of any area featured in this book.

Some prime areas for exploration, in addition to the ones featured here, are the primitive roads southeast of Pactola Reservoir, such as Forest

Roads (FR) 158 and 160, the roads south and northeast of Comanche Point Campground (mentioned in the Hell Canyon Loop), and the many paths crisscrossing the forest between Lead and Rapid City.

There is more private land interspersed among the Black Hills public lands than in the other national forests featured in this book. Numbered USFS roads are often gated shut to the public at the entrance to private lands. If you're going to explore roads not featured in this guide, check with USFS personnel to determine whether or not your planned route is entirely open to the public.

Although you might want to pick up additional maps for the national and state parks within the Black Hills area, all of the rides featured in this chapter are within the area encompassed by the Black Hills National Forest Visitors Map, available from Black Hills National Forest Supervisor's Office RR 2, Box 200, Custer, SD 57730, (605) 673-2251.

1 Wind Cave–Custer Loop

Riding surface:	pavement to smooth or slightly bumpy gravel and dirt
Beginning elevation:	4375 feet
Highest elevation:	4600 feet
Lowest elevation:	3600 feet
Distance:	23.3 miles
Relative difficulty:	moderate
Time to allow:	2 to 4 hours
Best time of year:	April through November
Best time of week:	any day
Supplemental map:	Black Hills National Forest Visitors Map

There is a lot to Wind Cave National Park besides Wind Cave. While there are 37 miles of passageways in Wind Cave (and it's a nice, cool [53° F] place to visit on a hot summer afternoon!) the above-ground portion of the park covers 28,060 acres! The natural prairie remaining here looks much as it did 200 years ago, providing visitors with a peek into the past.

If you're visiting the Black Hills in the middle of the summer, this is a ride you'll want to do early in the morning or late in the evening, when chances of viewing wildlife are better and temperatures are cooler. It can get *hot* out in the open grasslands: Temperatures exceeding 100°F are not uncommon.

Begin riding at the junction of State Highway 87 and National Park Service Road (NPS) 5, which is 8.5 miles north of the Wind Cave

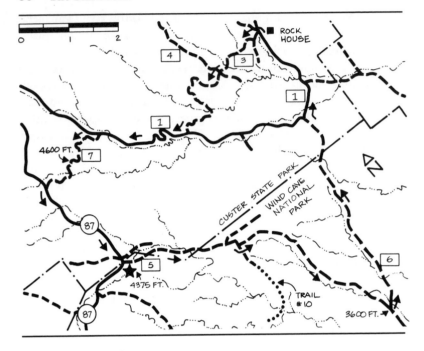

National Park Visitor Center, or 6 miles north of the Elk Mountain Campground. Ride southeast on NPS 5, which is a smooth, narrow gravel road. You start out on a gradual downhill, with timbered slopes rimming the open grasslands.

Bear left at 1.2 miles where a lesser-quality road goes right; you start uphill at 1.4. At 1.9 top out on a sweeping, grass-covered ridgetop. Pass by Trail 10 (hikers only) on the right at 2.6. At 3.0 the road changes from a red to a gray, rockier surface. The red surface resumes as you approach the edge of the ridge, and you begin down at 3.9 miles.

At 6.2 miles, at the bottom of this long descent, turn left onto NPS 6 just past a lone cottonwood (the other road continues straight ahead, onto private land). Here you begin riding uphill. If it's early morning or evening, the whir of your tires is bound to be accompanied by the melodic, flutelike song of the western meadowlark.

At 6.6 miles you top out temporarily and start down, then cross a creek at 7.1 and begin up again. It's gradually uphill until 8.7, where the climb steepens. You reach the ridgetop at 9.7 (at 9.6 is a nice grove of trees that would make a good picnic spot). At 9.9 miles the road enters Custer State Park and bottoms out at 10.0, where you have a short, steep uphill of about 0.1 mile.

At 10.7 turn right onto Custer State Park Road (CSP) 1 and begin a gradual uphill climb on very smooth blacktop. At 11.4 miles you top out and descend into a draw. At 12.8 (a distinctive rock house is on your right), make a sharp left turn onto gravel CSP 3. At this point you begin a series of roller-coaster hills until 14.2, where you ride straight through an intersection, continuing on CSP 3, and start up into a timbered draw.

You pass through a forest of ponderosa pine and bur oak, which has a markedly different feel to it than the open grasslands you've ridden through up to this point. Top out at 15.4, and then go down until 15.8 miles, where you cross a drainage and start up again. You begin down once more at 16.3, at 16.7 turn right onto paved CSP 1 and begin an uphill climb.

At 17.2 miles switchback left and then top out at 17.4 and begin down. At 18.9 turn left and begin riding uphill on gravel CSP 7, immediately after passing a prairie-dog town. You top out at 19.8 and, after a 0.3-mile level section, begin a steep descent. The road levels off at 20.5, and at 21.0 you turn left onto Hwy. 87. This road can carry a substantial amount of traffic during the summer, but sight distances are good and you're only on it for a little more than 2 miles.

At 23.2 re-enter Wind Cave National Park, returning to your point of origin at 23.3 miles.

2 Hell Canyon Loop

Riding surface:	pavement to primitive dirt
Beginning elevation:	5700 feet
Highest elevation:	6000 feet
Lowest elevation:	4500 feet
Distance:	26.8 miles
Relative difficulty:	moderate
Time to allow:	4 to 6 hours
Best time of year:	May through October
Best time of week:	any day
Supplemental map:	Black Hills National Forest Visitors Map

This loop includes a ride through Lithograph Canyon in Jewel Cave National Monument. Although the road through the canyon is open to the public, it is not shown on the National Park Service map.

Begin riding at the junction of Forest Road (FR) 273 and US Highway 16, 2.5 miles west of Comanche Point Campground (which is

6.5 miles west of the town of Custer). If starting this ride relatively late in the day, it might be a good idea to begin at mile 25.1 and do the 1.7 miles of highway riding first, as this is a narrow highway with fast-moving traffic which tends to become heavier in the afternoon. Head south on FR 273, a gradual downhill ride on a high-quality gravel road. During the first few miles, you pass through an area of rural homes.

At 4.8 miles, immediately after crossing a cattle guard, FR 274, a primitive forest path, goes right. For a shorter loop (approximately 18.5 miles), you can turn right here and hit FR 277 in about 5 miles (pick up the narrative below at mile 18.1).

Continue straight on FR 273 to accomplish the entire loop. At 7.6 miles you cross a cattle guard, going from private to USFS land, and the road curves left. At 7.8 you turn right onto an unsigned, primitive road not depicted on the Visitors Map. In 0.1 mile, bear right onto a less-traveled path and begin climbing. At 8.2, where you come to a fence corner, begin skirting the left side of the fence. At 8.5 *don't* go through

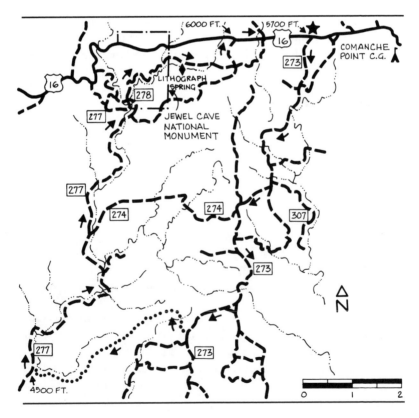

the gate, but bear left, following the main path, which weaves along the ridge. This is no major thoroughfare, but as long as you stay on the distinct, primitive road along the ridgetop, you're headed in the right direction.

At 10.2 miles you exit the woods and pass through a gate in a fence line (be sure to close the gate behind you). Bear left on the double-track path that follows the fence line. Here you begin a long stretch of riding through open grassland. At 10.6 bear right on the road that veers away from the fence line; a deep cattle trail continues along the fence. Wherever faced with a choice, continue bearing right on the main path through the grass. At 12.1 miles you start down into the timber.

At 12.2 pass through a USFS gate and descend a short, extremely steep hill on loose red rock. At the bottom of this, begin riding gradually downhill through a steep-sided, forested canyon. At 13.3 you pass through another USFS gate and then turn right at 13.4 onto FR 277 in beautiful, red-rock Hell Canyon. You've lost a great deal of elevation — about 1200 feet since the ride's beginning — and are now into the Red Valley "racetrack" which surrounds the Black Hills (see the introduction to this chapter). You now begin paying for this elevation loss: You'll climb about 1500 feet during the next 12 miles.

At 13.9 pass through a gate, and then another at 14.0 — you're skirting a private landing-strip, and there is a house off to the left. At 14.1 you pass through yet another gate. At 14.9 note a house about 0.2 mile to your right. You've left behind the red sandstone and are now riding through an area of limestone cliffs and shade-giving trees.

At 17.2 miles you pass a road which goes right to Waterdraw Springs (0.5 mile). At 18.1 FR 274 comes in from the right; the sign reads, "Pass Creek Road 273 - 5 mi." (this is where you'll join up if you took the shortcut mentioned at mile 4.8). You pass by another house on your right at 19.5.

At 21.1 miles ride straight onto FR 278 (FR 277 turns left; it joins US 16 in 1.5 miles - all uphill). At 21.3 you enter Jewel Cave National Monument. A lone picnic table is on your left just after entering the monument. At 21.7 you start riding amidst the multi-hued limestones of Lithograph Canyon. At 22.1, note on your left what looks for all the world like the "back door" to Jewel Cave. At 23.0 you exit Jewel Cave National Monument, re-entering Black Hills National Forest.

Lithograph Spring is on your right at 23.4, and at 24.5 miles the road curves hard left. At 25.1 you top out and turn right onto US 16, beginning the downhill ride back to your point of origin at 26.8.

3 Cement Ridge, Wyoming, Loop

Riding surface: smooth gravel to very rocky and bumpy
Beginning elevation: 5600 feet
Highest elevation: 6647 feet
Distance: 14.8 miles
Relative difficulty: hard
Time to allow: 3 to 5 hours
Best time of year: May through October
Best time of week: any day
Supplemental map: Black Hills National Forest Visitors Map

Begin this ride at Timon Campground, which is 5 miles west of
Spearfish Canyon Road (US Highway 14A) up Little Spearfish Canyon
Forest Road (FR) 222. You turn up FR 222 at the settlement of Savoy,
which is 13 miles west of Lead, or 14 miles south of Spearfish.

If you want to make this a little longer ride, you can begin before
Timon Campground. If you start and end the ride at Savoy, the total
mileage is 24.8; round-trip from Roughlock Falls would be 22.0; and
beginning and ending at Rod and Gun Campground would make the
total 18.2 miles. The riding from Savoy to Timon Campground is
pleasant and gently uphill, but be forewarned: Little Spearfish Canyon
is an extremely popular spot for sightseeing and fishing. Weekend traffic
jams on the lower stretches of FR 222 are not unheard of.

Beginning at Timon Campground, ride west on FR 222. The road
at this point is wide, with a well-packed gravel surface. At 0.3 the Rimrock
Trail trailhead is on your right. If it's the climax of autumn (generally mid-
to late-September here), the sight of these cliffsides ablaze with the fall
colors of aspens and other deciduous trees is guaranteed to take your
breath away!

At 1.2 miles, turn right at the T onto FR 134/222 (these roads
coincide for a short distance; FR 134 is a major road). At 1.5 turn left,
following FR 222; it drops below and temporarily parallels FR 134. It's
a good road but much narrower than the one you've just turned off of.
You commence climbing here.

At 2.0 you cross a cattle guard and ride into a wide-open "park"
entirely surrounded by aspen- and pine-covered ridges, reminiscent of
the high-elevation parks of Colorado and Wyoming. Begin riding
downhill at 2.2 miles. At 2.6 you bottom out at a cattle guard, climb for
0.1 mile, and then begin down again. At 3.1 miles you again bottom out,

The fire lookout atop Cement Ridge

and begin riding uphill straight ahead.

At 3.3 pass through an old ranch yard whose stout log buildings, still standing erect, are a stubborn reminder of the Black Hills' past. At 3.5 miles, still going up, you cross a cattle guard and begin a stretch of aspen-canopied road. You pass through an area in the 4.5-mile range which has been clear-cut in order to stimulate young aspen growth, which deer, elk, and other animals depend on as a food source. The climbing finally levels off at 4.7, and you begin a generally downhill section.

At 4.9 miles, FR 867 (designated FR 103 on the Visitors Map) goes off to your left; bear right, following FR 222. At 5.3 you turn left onto FR 802. Begin a steep downhill which is quite rocky and bumpy. At 5.5 you can see, above and to your left, the lookout on Cement Ridge — that's where you'll be soon!

At 6.0 miles, just before a cattle guard, turn left onto an unsigned road, which heads up into a steep drainage. (As an alternative, you can continue straight across the cattle guard and turn left at the T at 6.5 — this will bring you, at 7.8, to the point described below.)

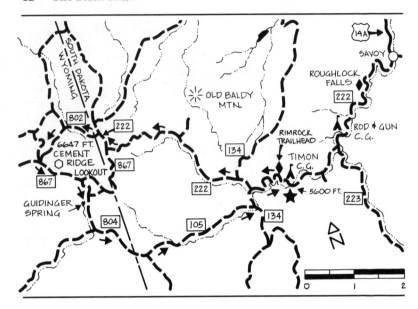

At the top of this very steep climb, at 6.8, you arrive at a four-way junction. Go straight up the steep four-wheel-drive road, which becomes quite rocky; you'll probably have to walk portions of it. At 7.4 miles you arrive, with very tired legs, at the Cement Ridge Lookout. The views back into the Black ·Hills and west out onto the Wyoming prairie make the climbing worth the trouble, however. Up here along the ridge would be a good place to camp if you're equipped for it. (Be sure you have plenty of water along, as there is no convenient water source.)

Continuing southeast on the same road, crest a slight bump in the terrain and then start down along the ridge. At 8.4 miles turn right onto an unsigned but high-quality road. This is a very steep, smooth, fun downhill. At 9.1 miles pass Guidinger Spring off to your right. At 9.4 turn left at the T onto FR 804. This is also a narrow, high-quality road.

At 9.6 miles cross a cattle guard and continue climbing steeply. At 10.0 you crest a divide and start down through a forest of large ponderosa pine and aspen. At 10.5 you re-enter South Dakota; at 10.7 bear left onto FR 105 at the T (the sign here reads, "Savoy 8 mi."). At 11.5 you cross a cattle guard; in another 0.3 mile you pass through an old abandoned farmstead.

At 13.5 miles turn left onto FR 134 (the same gravel "superhigh-way" you were on once before), and then turn right onto signed "Timon Canyon Rd./222" at 13.7, still heading downhill. At 14.8 you're back at Timon Campground.

4 Black Hills Experimental Forest

Riding surface: smooth to slightly rocky
Beginning elevation: 5400 feet
Highest elevation: 6000 feet
Distance: variable
Relative difficulty: easy
Time to allow: 1 to 4 hours
Best time of year: May through October
Best time of week: weekend
Supplemental map: Black Hills National Forest Visitors Map

The Black Hills Experimental Forest is a thickly forested area which doesn't offer a lot of long-range vistas. However, it has several redeeming features. Because the forest is in the Central Plateau, the roads drain well, so you could ride here during or shortly after rains without becoming bogged down in mud. The relatively high elevation and the shade provided by the heavy forest make this a good place to ride on a hot day. Finally, the system of roads here is laid out in such a manner that it looks like it was intentionally designed for mountain biking and cross-country skiing!

Although there are plenty of hills, the ups and downs are generally well graded and the road surfaces uniform, providing few surprises. This

From Cement Ridge you can gaze out across the Black Hills to the distant Wyoming prairie.

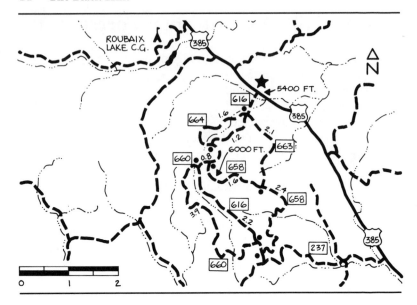

is the perfect place to bring the family to spend a morning riding.

The road system has been reproduced on the accompanying map, including interim mileages, so you can plan the ride and distance you want to do. In addition to the primary routes depicted on the accompanying map, many primitive logging paths depart from the main roads.

To get to the Black Hills Experimental Forest, go 16 miles west on Rimrock Drive (State Highway 44) from Rapid City, then approximately 8 miles northwest on US Highway 385. Turn left (south) onto Forest Road 616 and park at the four-way junction (0.5 mile from the turnoff). If you're arriving from the north, the turnoff to FR 616 is about 17 miles southeast of both Lead and Deadwood on US 385. A good spot to base out of is Roubaix Lake Campground, which is about 2.5 miles northwest of the turnoff to FR 616.

2

The Bighorn Mountains

The Bighorn Mountains are the first alpine range that many folks traveling from the East or Midwest will encounter en route to Yellowstone Park. Most people don't expect to see mountains before Yellowstone and are surprised by the grand scale of the range.

The Bighorns rise sharply from the surrounding plains and extend from northern Wyoming into southern Montana. The Bighorn National Forest covers 1,141,936 acres in an area 80 miles long, north to south, by 30 miles wide. The highest point in the range, Cloud Peak, at 13,165 feet, is namesake for the Cloud Peak Wilderness, which makes up more than 10 percent of the national forest. This wilderness, which is entirely above 8500 feet in elevation, contains no fewer than 260 lakes and 45 miles of fishable streams.

The towns of Buffalo and Sheridan, which lie along the eastern slope of the Bighorns, are connected by Interstate 90. Considering the bucolic nature of the countryside which separates these communities today, it's hard to imagine the turmoil that the area has seen in the past. The "Bloody Bozeman" Trail passed along here, and the ruins of Fort Phil Kearny — by the Indians, the most hated military outpost along the Bozeman — are today being restored. A rich collection of artifacts from the area's past can be found at the Jim Gatchell Museum in Buffalo. In Sheridan are the Trail End Museum and the Bradford Brinton Memorial Ranch. These portray the period of the late 1800s, when wealthy cattle barons were lords of the local lands.

The terrain of the Bighorns is more rolling than that of the big Wyoming ranges to the west and south, such as the Absaroka and the Wind River ranges. Because the Bighorns have such a great total relief (Cloud Peak is more than 9000 feet above both Sheridan, on the east side of the mountains, and Worland, which lies along the western slope), they also contain a vast array of life-zones, or environments. You'll ride in hard, dry desert canyons much like those of southeast Utah, and through wet alpine meadows laced and scented with wildflowers representing every color in the spectrum.

The southern end of the Bighorns contains what is commonly considered the grandest scenery of the range. The lakes and high peaks, many of which are within the Cloud Peak Wilderness, are concentrated here. But, while the northern reaches tend to be high, dry, and more barren than the southern parts of the forest, they also see substantially less use by recreationists.

Some good areas to explore by bike other than those featured here include the Canyon Park-Powder River area just south of Powder River Pass; Forest Roads 422201 and 301301, which will take you from near the Medicine Lodge State Archaeological Site (see Ride 4) to Shell Creek Ranger Station, through some spectacular high regions; and the country between the Bighorn River and Cookstove Basin, at the northern end of the forest (including Boyd Ridge, Crater Ridge, and the road to Red and Willow springs).

Finally, an attraction which should not be missed is the Medicine Wheel. This stone feature, constructed by prehistoric Native Americans, is located high atop a windblown ridge, surrounded by stunted pines and castlelike rock formations, at the breathtaking elevation of 9640 feet. The sight naturally leads one to speculate as to its purpose and significance. (As if to demonstrate his superiority over primitive people, modern man has chosen to build a UFO-looking radar facility atop the even higher Medicine Mountain, in clear view of the Medicine Wheel.) The 11-mile round-trip ride here from Bald Mountain Campground is quite breathtaking in its own right. The campground, and the turnoff to the Medicine Wheel, are on the northwest edge of the Bighorn National Forest, midway between the town of Lovell and Burgess Junction on US Highway 14A.

Two miles farther up FR 123401 (which is signed FR 12 on the ground), beyond the Medicine Wheel, is a system of old logging roads in the Elk Springs area. These roads, now closed to motorized traffic, are recommended for mountain biking by the USFS. The roads are not shown on the USFS maps, but are easy to find — and worth finding, for they offer some really fun riding through high-elevation spruce forest.

The supplemental maps for the area are available from: Bighorn National Forest Supervisor's Office, 1969 S. Sheridan Ave., Sheridan, WY 82801 (307) 672-0751.

It is important to note that the Bighorn National Forest is in the midst of a road designation change. They are switching from a six-digit system to a much simpler two- and three-digit system. The roads you ride on will not necessarily be signed the same on the maps and on the ground. However, this should not present a major problem as long as you correlate the mileages given in the narrative with the mileages shown on your odometer.

Give the following rides a try, and see if you don't want to explore even more in the Bighorns!

1 Firebox Park Out and Back

Riding surface: smooth to extremely rutted and rocky
Beginning elevation: 7880 feet
Highest elevation: 8160 feet
Lowest elevation: 7020 feet
Distance: 19.0 miles
Relative difficulty: hard
Time to allow: 4 to 7 hours
Best time of year: June through September
Best time of week: any day
Supplemental maps: Bighorn National Forest Visitors Map, Bighorn National Forest Travel Plan Map

This ride begins on rutted four-wheel-drive roads, but also involves some trail riding. Although portions of these trails are not open to motorcycles, the USFS recommends them for mountain biking. This is a very low-use area of the forest. Some locals maintain that this Firebox Park country is more like wilderness than the Cloud Peak Wilderness is. While it is not quite as magnificent, hardly anyone visits here compared to the hordes who flock into the Cloud Peak area.

From Buffalo, go about 12 miles west on US Highway 16 and turn north into North Fork Picnic Ground (Middle Fork Campground, just 1 mile farther up Hwy. 16, is a good place to camp). You can begin the ride at the picnic ground, but it's probably a better idea to drive the next 2.6 miles up FR 19 and park at the roadhead of FR 474313 (called FR 474411 on the maps). This ride is long and tiring enough without the hard uphill from the picnic ground.

If, at the 15.5 mile point below, you were to go straight through the gate, you'd pass onto the private property of the Paradise Ranch, which is owned by the Apache Oil Company. This is a multi-million-dollar dude ranch. It may be worth your while, before beginning this ride, to drive to the ranch, which is a mile farther up the road from where you want to begin riding, and ask the ranch personnel if they mind your riding across their property. If you're granted permission, it will save you 1.8 miles of riding (and 3.5 miles of backtracking). Do not do it without permission, however!

Begin riding up FR 474313 (sign here reads, "French Creek Swamp $1\frac{1}{2}$ mi."). After a 0.1-mile climb, go down a short hill and through

Heading down into the Rock Creek drainage from Firebox Park

a gate at 0.2 mile. At the fork just beyond the gate, bear right toward French Creek Swamp, and begin a stiff climb to 0.5, where the grade lessens and you enter the woods. At 0.6 mile you must either ford Four Lakes Ditch or walk across a precarious set of logs (this crossing is slated to be bridged prior to 1990). Once across the ditch, you begin a very rocky uphill; be cautious of your pedal clearance — keep them horizontal as much as possible.

At 1.1 you begin a level-to-gently-downhill stretch; you're still in a pine and spruce forest. At 1.6 you come into the French Creek Swamp area, which is extremely messy. For the next 0.3 mile or so, you will need to do some walking in order to stay on higher ground and out of the muck. Motorized ORVs have done a lot of damage to this wetland. Other than the road corridor, however, it's a beautiful meadow with good views of high peaks in the nearby wilderness area.

At 2.1 miles you arrive at the back of a sign. Bear right here toward "Paradise Ranch/Keno Creek." At 3.1 you come to a point where a faint trail goes down to the right; bear left on the path which goes up through the woods. At 3.5, after a 0.3-mile descent, roll into a big, grassy bowl, where there is a four-way junction; turn left toward Rock Creek. Just after turning onto this trail you pass by a sign that reads, "HF Bar Ranch 10." Here you begin a smooth, fun downhill.

At 4.6 miles you cross a small creek; you're still in open bottomland with timbered slopes on both sides. At 5.1 you once again cross a small creek. (Just before crossing it, you'll note a primitive campsite in a grove of trees on your right. You could ride to this point with gear and set up camp, then do the rest of the route as a day ride, returning here to spend the night.)

At 5.3 miles bear right at the fork, *away* from the trail to Gem Lake. At 5.4 you come to your first crossing of Rock Creek; walk your bike across. At 5.9 there's a second crossing of Rock Creek, and at 6.5 you cross a small feeder stream. The trail winds gently downstream through the woods; it is ridable for the most part, with fun technical sections provided by the many roots and rocks.

At 6.6 pass through a USFS gate. At 7.0 you cross Rock Creek for the third time. At 7.1 cross another feeder stream and another at 7.4, after which you arrive at a fork, where you turn right toward Firebox Park, and cross Rock Creek, at 7.5. The next 0.3 mile is very steep as you leave the creek bottom; it levels off and becomes ridable at 7.8 miles. At 7.9 you begin a nice downhill through an aspen grove, and then start uphill at 8.1. This is prime elk habitat, so keep on the lookout.

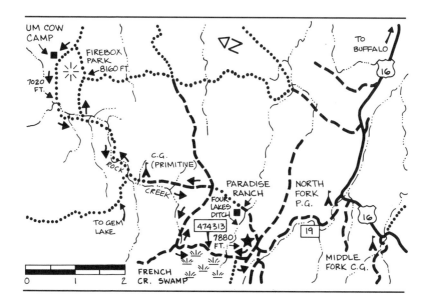

At 8.5 miles temporarily top out on the side of a ridge, then continue up at 8.6. At 8.7 miles you arrive at a saddle which provides wonderful views. This is the spot for lunch and photos.

Continuing down the other side of the saddle, you come to a post stuck in the ground at 9.1. You're now in Firebox Park. Go straight ahead, and at a second post, at 9.2, turn acute left and begin following a good trail which leads to the other side of the knob which you skirted coming down off the saddle. Just ride around the knob, keeping it on your left side. At 9.3, after a short uphill, begin down on a smooth, single-track trail. The views of the Bighorn peaks straight ahead are captivating — you'd better stop to take a good look, or you might crash!

At 9.6 you encounter a precarious slope, which you'll want to walk your bike down. At 9.7 cross a small stream, and at 9.9 you arrive at a cabin which is signed, "UM Cow Camp." Turn left in front of the cabin and find the trail, which enters the woods, by watching for blazes on the trees. At 10.1 pass through a primitive campsite, and at 10.3 you come alongside Rock Creek once again.

At 10.8 miles there's a 0.1-mile section of big rocks which leads to your fifth crossing of Rock Creek. At 11.5 you're back at the point where earlier you departed from Rock Creek, making the loop through Firebox Park a total of 4 miles. Backtrack from this point on, through Rock Creek a sixth, seventh and, finally, eighth time, at 13.4 miles. At 13.7 you return to the previously mentioned campsite (bringing the total mileage of the loop from there and back to 8.6).

At 15.5 miles you return to the four-way junction you first encountered at 3.5 miles. Turn right here and go out the way you came in, bringing the total mileage for your ride to 19.0.

2 East Tensleep Lake Loop

Riding surface:	pavement to rough and rocky
Beginning elevation:	8680 feet
Highest elevation:	9720 feet
Lowest elevation:	8070 feet
Distance:	17.0 miles
Relative difficulty:	moderate
Time to allow:	3 to 6 hours
Best time of year:	July through September
Best time of week:	any day
Supplemental maps:	Bighorn National Forest Visitors Map, Bighorn National Forest Travel Plan Map

East Tensleep Lake and the distant Cloud Peak Wilderness

This ride is recommended by the Tensleep District of the Bighorn National Forest. It's a gem.

The word Tensleep reportedly derives from a creek crossing on the old Bridger Trail. To the Indians, this spot was ten days (or "sleeps") from Fort Laramie to the southeast, as well as ten sleeps from Yellowstone Park to the northwest.

The ride begins at Sitting Bull Campground, which is 0.7 mile north of US Highway 16 from a point 20 miles northeast of Tensleep and 45 miles southwest of Buffalo. From the campground, ride back down the smooth gravel road to the highway, and turn left onto it at 0.7 mile. After 0.3 mile of uphill, turn left onto Forest Road 430, which is also designated 513111. Here you begin a steep uphill.

At 1.7, in the middle of the 1975 Meadowlark Burn, you hit a "walker." Since you have to dismount anyway, steal a look at the views behind you of Meadowlark Lake and the Bighorn Basin beyond. At 1.8 you can begin riding again. At 2.1 miles is a very short walker, after which you're rewarded with an all-too-brief downhill. At 2.3 you begin a steep, but ridable, uphill stretch. The old burn is quite ghastly, but the surrounding views are superb.

After a couple more short ups and downs, you leave the burn behind at 2.7 as you coast into a big meadow. At 2.8, near a footbridge across East Tensleep Creek, you begin winding upstream along the left side of the creek. At 3.2 pass by a fenced-off section of stream which was enclosed by the Youth Conservation Corps (Y.C.C.) in 1986 to protect the riparian habitat and to demonstrate that overgrazing of the meadow by domestic sheep was having an adverse effect on the area. At 3.5 climb stiffly up onto a glacial moraine, and then begin a section of short ups and downs.

At 4.9 you arrive at a fork at the foot of a steep hill. The right fork, which goes to Maybelle Lake and Lake McLain, goes into the wilderness; you bear left at the sign reading "E. Tensleep Lk." on the more beaten path. The next mile is a rough and rocky uphill. A strong rider will be able to ride most of it. At 6.0, on top, arrive at a T where you turn right and immediately come to another fork. Bear left here, and pass through a distinct campsite, which even has an outhouse!

At 6.2 turn right along the path which parallels the lake's outlet creek. You'll see an old, deteriorated bridge off to your left. Continue upstream to the boulder-covered slope where the creek falls from the small lake below East Tensleep Lake. To cross the slope shoulder your bicycle and haul it up over the boulders. Walk across the log spanning the outlet stream right where it flows from the lake. For a good look at East Tensleep Lake, park your bike and walk around the bank of the small lake for a short ways. From this log crossing, look down to your left across the meadow and spot a sign — head for this sign, staying on as high of ground as possible.

From this sign — which reads "Highline Trail"— at 6.4 miles, you'll see another one just beyond, up in the woods. Go to it, turn left, and start down. You can ride to 7.0, where you hit a short section of steeper downhill, which you should walk. At the bottom of this, you come to a trail sign. Bear left, *away* from the Highline Trail, toward a post and some rock cairns, and walk the short stretch through a boulder field.

At 7.5 miles the trail makes a sharp left — at this point it is somewhat indistinct, so keep a close eye out for blazes on the trees. At 7.9 the trail hooks right and is easy to lose — again, watch for blazes! At 8.4 you enter an open park and arrive at a junction. At the sign, bear straight toward "Tyrell Ranger Station" (if you're tired and want to take a shortcut, it's about 2 miles back to Sitting Bull Campground if you turn left here, toward US 16).

Drop through the woods on a smooth trail, and enter a meadow at 8.6. Spot a pole in the meadow, and head for it, bearing to the right of the timber. You hit a second pole at 8.7 and then pick up the trail as it leads back into the woods. At 8.9 cross a little creek after a steep downhill, then pass through a willow thicket. The next 0.5 mile is a very pleasant,

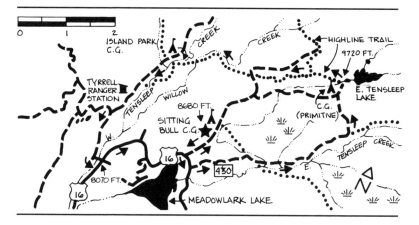

winding downhill through the woods.

From 9.4 to 9.9 miles, you have a steady downhill, some of it quite technically demanding due to roots and switchbacks on this steep slope, which contains a great deal of blow-down. You have a little uphill, then a downhill to Willow Creek, which you cross on a dilapidated but usable bridge, at 10.1 miles. After a short, bumpy section of exposed tree roots, the trail becomes baby-bottom smooth. At 10.3 you crest a knob and coast out into a meadow at 10.4 miles. Meander through this meadow, and brush up against West Tensleep Creek. Across the creek and adjacent meadow, you can see Island Park Campground through the trees.

At 10.6 miles climb back into the woods. At 11.4 watch for blazes, as the trail veers right through an area of boulders where it is easy to lose. There's a bit of walking necessary through these large rocks. At 11.5, immediately after the boulders, arrive at the back of a sign. Turn right at this junction, and cross West Tensleep Creek. You'd have to search a long while in order to find a mountain stream any prettier than the one you're crossing on this Cadillac of a footbridge!

Upon rolling off the bridge, follow the blazes on the trees to the left, through a rocky streambed (which was dry in early September, when this route was covered). Above the streambed, at 11.6, bear right, crossing the primitive road perpendicularly (this is a "no vehicles" road), heading straight into the woods. Look hard for blazes — they're sometimes difficult to spot, but there is an apparent swath through the woods. Regardless, even if you do get off-trail here, just keep heading straight and you'll come to the main road. (This trail looked as if it had been recently re-routed in the fall of 1987. It will likely be better-signed and more worn in the future.)

At 11.7 exit the woods into a small clearing, and bear right alongside the woods (don't cross the meadow). At 11.9 you come out of the woods, turn left onto a major gravel road, and start down. At 12.3 miles you cross a cattle guard and then pass by Tyrell Work Center. At 12.7 you ride over another cattle guard and start a steep downhill. Cross West Tensleep Creek at 13.9, turn left onto US 16, and start uphill.

The road levels off at 15.9 miles as you skirt Meadowlark Lake. At 16.3 turn left and ride back up to Sitting Bull Campground, at 17.0 miles.

3 Tensleep Canyon Loop

Riding surface: pavement to smooth gravel
Beginning elevation: 5275 feet
Highest elevation: 7490 feet
Distance: 15.6 miles
Relative difficulty: moderate
Time to allow: 2 to 3 hours
Best time of year: May through October
Best time of week: weekdays
Supplemental maps: Bighorn National Forest Visitors Map, Big-
                       horn National Forest Travel Plan Map

Begin this ride at Tensleep Creek Campground, 1.3 miles up Forest Road 26, which meets US Highway 16 at a point 7 miles east of Tensleep. This loop encompasses the old and the new highways through Tensleep Canyon. You can ride it in either a clockwise or counter-clockwise direction and be rewarded with fantastic views either way. You may prefer the counter-clockwise route, as you're riding *up* the old road, so you spend more time on it. The downhill portion, which is equal in distance but much shorter in time, will be on the new highway, with motorized

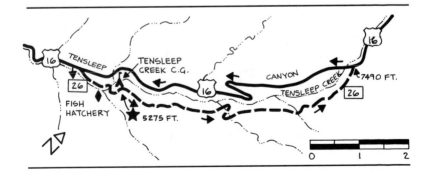

The view down Tensleep Canyon, with the old road on the left and the new highway on the right

traffic. Tensleep Canyon is considered one of the greatest scenic attractions in all of Wyoming, and you'll soon understand why!

Leaving Tensleep Creek Campground, turn left, continuing up FR 26. At 0.1 pass through an open USFS gate and then switchback right, to be greeted with views deep into Leigh Canyon. At 0.4 you're looking down on the tops of the campground's cottonwoods. Keep climbing, pausing often to enjoy the views of Tensleep Creek below. At 3.1 you switchback right, then left again at 3.4. The old paved surface is quite broken up and potholed in some places.

At 4.4 pass through an area of nearly perfect "basking" rocks — their only drawback is a somewhat bumpy surface. Packing along a foam pad will solve this little problem. Stretch out and become a fat toad on a hot rock!

The old paved surface soon deteriorates into gravel. The views and photo opportunities in the 5.0 area are exquisite. Look across the canyon and behind you at the switchbacks on the new highway — that's what you'll be riding down! You're in country that is largely open sage hillsides with timber along the cliffs and aspen filling in the draws. Continuing your climb, you arrive at the junction with the new highway at 6.5 miles; turn left onto the highway, and begin the speedy downhill cruise. The road is quite wide and offers pleasant riding conditions, even with the sometimes heavy tourist traffic it carries, which tends to increase on weekends.

At 14.3 miles turn left back onto FR 26 onto very smooth pavement. At 15.4 you cross Tensleep Creek and pass by the Tensleep Fish Hatchery on your right. Constructed of logs in 1938 and still in operation, this is one of the state's most productive hatcheries. Visitors are welcome. At 15.6 miles you're back at Tensleep Creek Campground.

4 Dry Fork Medicine Lodge Creek Out and Back

Riding surface:	smooth sand to somewhat bumpy
Beginning elevation:	4780 feet
Highest elevation:	5480 feet
Distance:	9 miles
Relative difficulty:	easy
Time to allow:	1 to 2 hours
Best time of year:	June through November; road closed to vehicles December 1 to June 1 for wildlife protection
Best time of week:	any day
Supplemental maps:	Bighorn National Forest Visitors Map, Bighorn National Forest Travel Plan Map

This ride takes you onto hallowed ground. It's a good ride to do on a day when the weather is threatening. It can be relatively nice at this elevation even when it's storming in the higher country. The ride begins and ends at the Medicine Lodge State Archaeological Site Campground.

To get to the site, you first have to locate Hyattville, Wyoming. Hyattville, population 100, is 25 miles northwest of Tensleep on the Nowood River Road; or, coming from the other direction, it's 22 miles east of Manderson on State Highway 31. Once you get to Hyattville, follow the signs to "Archaeological Site," 6 miles north and east of town. The pleasant campground is situated on the banks of Medicine Lodge Creek and is shaded by huge, old cottonwoods that smell sweet as candy in the spring. Due to its remote location, the campground sees relatively little use.

From the campground, ride your bike north up the road toward the archaeological site. Curve left, then right around the superintendent's home, and arrive at the site at 0.5 mile. These sandstone cliffs had been known for decades for the petroglyphs and pictographs which decorate their face. But major archaeological excavations in the 1970s uncovered

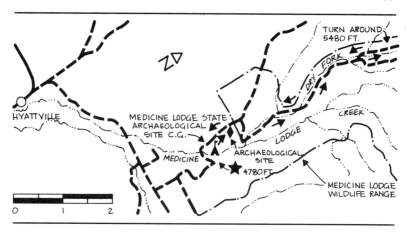

evidence of 60 individual cultural levels. From bottom to top, evidence was unearthed of Paleo Indians, who camped in the area 10,000 years ago, to the Crow Indians who lived here when the white man finally arrived over a century ago. The summer shade and winter warmth provided by the big yellow cliffs made this a natural campground for the parade of different peoples who, down through time, called this spot home.

As you leave the site and ride into the Dry Fork Canyon, consider this: 100 centuries ago, men walked where you're riding. That is about 99 centuries before the first white man set foot in the area! This is an easy ride which should be taken slowly and humbly. Admire the surrounding sandstone cliffs and caves, feel the sharp pungency of sage filling your nostrils, and respect the spirits of the Ancients, which undoubtedly you will sense are still dwelling here. It is a special, holy place.

Continue through the site, bearing right on the main road. After crossing the Dry Fork you bear left. Ride straight ahead at 0.6 rather than turning right into the group campsites. At 0.7 you pass through an open gate. The canyon you're riding into is part of the Medicine Lodge Wildlife Habitat Management Unit, which consists of more than 12,000 acres of state and BLM lands. This range provides important winter habitat for large herds of mule deer and elk.

You're riding on a smooth double-track road, which becomes a little steeper and rockier at 0.9 mile. At 1.1 you again cross the Dry Fork on a good bridge and pass through a gate. If the weather has been dry, you may discover sections where the road is so powdery that it can cause steering problems. If this is the case, try riding on the center ridge. At 1.9

you ride through the Dry Fork bed. Stop often to scan the juniper-studded slopes (with binoculars, if you have them) for wildlife.

At 3.5 miles cross back over to the left side of the drainage, and ride over a cattle guard at 3.6. A large side canyon, inviting you to explore on foot, joins in at this point (do keep an eye out for rattlesnakes and prickly pear cactus!). At 3.8 miles you "hit the wall," as the road you've been on becomes prohibitively steep. (This four-wheel-drive road continues up and finally out of the canyon and eventually climbs into the high Bighorns. Some good multi-day trips would be possible by beginning on this road, but the radical grades preclude all but the hardiest of riders.)

Where the wall starts up, bear left on the cattle trail across the Dry Fork and start riding on the old, grassy roadbed along the left side of the creek. This road takes you right along the base of the cliffs, past several overhangs and intriguing, small caves. You can continue along it to an old bridge abutment at 4.5 miles, where the road becomes overgrown and deteriorated.

At this point, turn around and return to the campground, which you re-enter at 9.0 miles, having experienced the magic of Dry Fork Canyon.

5 Hunt Mountain Point to Point

Riding surface:	generally smooth gravel
Beginning elevation:	8950 feet
Highest elevation:	10,020 feet
Distance:	22.4 miles
Relative difficulty:	moderate
Time to allow:	2 to 5 hours
Best time of year:	July through September
Best time of week:	any day
Supplemental maps:	Bighorn National Forest Visitors Map, Bighorn National Forest Travel Plan Map

Begin just east of Granite Pass, which is 35 miles east of Greybull on US Highway 14, or 50 miles west of Sheridan. You'll need to either arrange for a shuttle or hitch a ride back to your car; or you could turn this in to a very long day ride. By doing the 22-mile ride outlined here, then riding on paved US Highway 14A to Burgess Junction, and south on Hwy. 14 back to Granite Pass, the entire distance would measure about 45 miles. And they are 45 hilly miles, almost entirely above 8000 feet in elevation.

Mule deer on the Hunt Mountain Point to Point

From Granite Pass, drive north on Hwy. 14 for 0.2 mile and begin the ride at the junction with Forest Road 10/Hunt Mountain Road (designated FR 122212 on the USFS Travel Plan Map). Ride west on this smooth gravel road, crossing a cattle guard at 0.1 mile. Here you begin riding uphill through sage-covered slopes.

At the top of a long uphill, at 2.4, you cross a cattle guard and begin down. There are good views of the distant Bighorn peaks behind you. Beginning at 2.6 you ride through a timbered stretch for 0.2 mile. You have a couple relatively short ups and downs then, at 4.1, you begin a gradual downhill which bottoms out at 5.4, where you start up again. If you look at the map, you'll see that you're crossing from side to side of the high divide which defines the Big Horn–Sheridan County Line. Granite Pass, near the point where you began this ride, is atop this same long ridgeline.

Begin another series of 0.2- to 0.5-mile ups and downs, passing some exceptional viewpoints in the 7.2-mile range. At 9.5 miles you pass

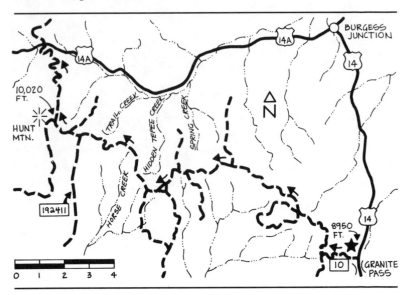

the signed Spring Creek drainage on your right, and at 11.0, atop a high point, you have good Bighorn views on your left. Continuing this roller-coaster ride, pass by Hidden Tipi Creek on your right at 12.0, and at 12.3, note FR 192411 on your left, which goes out to Sunlight Mesa. That route is recommended by the USFS as a good, but hard mountain-bike ride.

You'll find that the country you're riding through is not particularly gorgeous — in some regards, in fact, it is rather bleak. It's high, dry, and desertlike. But the "fun factor" of this undulating road along with the long-range vistas you're afforded in all directions combine to make this a ride that shouldn't be missed.

Continuing with a series of short ups and downs, you pass through a small spruce stand at 13.5 miles and then ride past Horse Creek on your left at 14.2. At 15.2 you ride by Trail Creek on your right and begin a longer uphill which tops out at 16.4. After a brief downhill section, you begin a very long climb which crests at 19.4, at which point you begin a 3-mile downhill. At 20.0 you switchback to the right, and then to the left.

At 20.8, after passing through another spruce stand, switchback to the right, and then again to the left. Following a set of S curves and a switchback to the right, you arrive at Hwy. 14A at 22.4 miles. How about another ride on the roller coaster?!

3
Yellowstone Country

Yellowstone National Park and the surrounding country are among the most beautiful and wildlife-abundant regions on earth. The trails within the park are off-limits to mountain biking, as they should be, but some of the routes in this chapter feature low-traffic gravel roads inside Yellowstone. And there is equally beautiful country outside the park's boundaries, in the Gallatin, Custer, Shoshone, Bridger-Teton, and Targhee national forests. Within these forests you'll discover an abundance of roads and jeep trails ideally suited for mountain-bike travel. Here, there are mountain-biking routes — some within a stone's throw of Yellowstone Park's boundaries — where you won't see another person during a full day's outing.

Four of the five entrances to Yellowstone Park are represented by the rides in this chapter: the North Entrance (Yankee Jim Point to Point), the West Entrance (Divide Ride Loop), the South Entrance (Grassy Lake

Fly-fishing on the Lewis River, Yellowstone National Park. Nancy McCoy photo

Ducks on the water at dusk, Yellowstone Lake's Bridge Bay

Point to Point), and the Northeast Entrance (Lulu Loop). There is no ride featured near the East Entrance because the available riding there is limited; after leaving the park, the highway heading east to Cody runs through a narrow corridor surrounded by wilderness — the Absaroka Wilderness to the north and the Washakie Wilderness to the south of the highway.

Supplemental maps for each ride in this chapter are listed at the beginning of the ride description. The maps are available from:

Bridger-Teton National Forest Supervisor's Office
340 North Cache Street
Jackson, WY 83001
(307) 733-2752

Custer National Forest Supervisor's Office
P.O. Box 2556
Billings, MT 59103
(406) 657-6361

Gallatin National Forest Supervisor's Office
P.O. Box 130
Bozeman, MT 59771
(406) 587-6701

Targhee National Forest Supervisor's Office
420 North Bridge St.
St. Anthony, ID 83445
(208) 624-3151

1 Yankee Jim Point to Point

Riding surface:	generally smooth gravel
Beginning elevation:	6250 feet
Highest elevation:	6250 feet
Lowest elevation:	4930 feet
Distance:	26.4 miles
Relative difficulty:	easy
Time to allow:	2 to 4 hours
Best time of year:	May through October
Best time of week:	any day
Supplemental map:	Gallatin National Forest Visitors Map

This ride begins on a gravel road *within* Yellowstone National Park, in the town of Mammoth Hot Springs. It takes you out, back in, and again out of the park and along the west side of the Yellowstone River, which flows northward out of the high country en route to its confluence with the Missouri River. The ride penetrates a canyon which, for more than a quarter century, was guarded by Yankee Jim, who carved out the road that still bears his name and owned the only stopping place for travelers in the upper Yellowstone Valley.

Yankee Jim is not around today, but another keeper now guards some of the country through which this ride passes. The Church Universal and Triumphant (CUT), a religious organization from southern California, has taken up residence on the Royal Teton Ranch, which borders Yellowstone National Park. Public access through the ranch is limited to the main road, a fact reinforced by numerous no-trespassing signs.

To begin, ride onto the gravel road behind the Mammoth Hot Springs Hotel. (This one-way road is signed "Gardiner 5 miles.") After a 0.3-mile uphill, the road flattens out. At 0.6 begin a long, smooth downhill. The pleasure of the descent is enhanced by the fact that it's a one-way road, so you can be quite sure you won't meet any cars coming up (very few motorized vehicles negotiate this road, even in the correct direction). The smooth road winds down an exposed, sage-covered slope high above the main highway and the riffling waters of the mighty Yellowstone. You'll likely spot the telltale brown and white of pronghorn antelope along the roadsides.

At 1.4 you pass through a small stand of pine and aspen. The downhill bottoms out at 3.5, and at 4.0 you arrive at the highway at the North Entrance to Yellowstone Park. Carefully turn left onto this

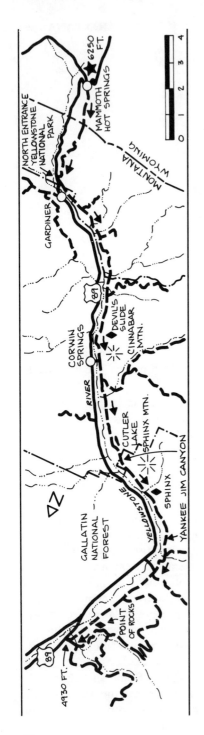

6250 FT.

MAMMOTH HOT SPRINGS

NORTH ENTRANCE
YELLOWSTONE NATIONAL PARK

GARDINER

MONTANA
WYOMING

89

CORWIN SPRINGS

DEVIL'S SLIDE

CINNABAR MTN.

RIVER

CUTLER LAKE

SPHINX MTN.

SPHINX

YANKEE JIM CANYON

YELLOWSTONE

N

GALLATIN NATIONAL FOREST

POINT OF ROCKS

89

4930 FT.

0 1 2 3 4

highway. Go through the rock archway at 4.6 miles, then immediately turn left off the highway, following the rock wall. At 4.7, at the end of the wall, bear left, riding behind the Gardiner High School athletic field.

At 4.8 miles you re-enter Yellowstone National Park; you resume riding on a gravel road at 4.9. It's wider than the previous gravel road and is no longer one-way. The terrain is rolling to 5.6 miles, where it flattens out as you pedal along the second bench above the Yellowstone River. It's quite desertlike here. If you're fortunate enough to be riding during or just after a rain shower, you'll enjoy the invigorating scent of juniper and sage.

At 9.0 miles leave Yellowstone Park and begin skirting the Royal Teton Ranch. At 9.6 you pass by the ranch office. At 10.7 miles note the beautifully folded rainbow rock of Devil's Slide on your left. At 12.3 miles you pass by the bridge which crosses the Yellowstone River to Corwin Springs. Bear left, away from the bridge, at this point. (You could cross here and ride back to Mammoth Hot Springs on the highway, making a loop of about 24 miles, but you'll miss some of the nicest riding!)

At 13.0 miles bear right along the river, as the road to the left goes up to the ranch headquarters. The road becomes a little narrower past this point. At 13.7 miles you cross a creek; bear left, then follow the road right through the Royal Teton Ranch. At 14.0 you pass a long, private landing-strip. At 14.8 miles begin ascending; the road becomes narrower, with a grass strip down the middle. Top out at 15.3, with nice views down to the river. At 15.7 you pass by Cutler Lake on the left, then begin down at 15.9.

At 16.8 bottom out on the floodplain; enter the Gallatin National Forest at 17.1, where the road becomes even more primitive. Here you're coming in to the heart of Yankee Jim Canyon, with big, yellow and red rock walls on your left and a cooling cottonwood grove lining the river on your right. There are nice spots for camping here. In this area of public land, you could hike up higher onto the rocks and be rewarded with terrific views of the river below. It's a fine spot for meditation: The soothing wind purrs through the cottonwoods, and the Yellowstone — now a large, wide river — hisses by, whispering the secrets of nature.

At 18.0 miles you can go either way at the fork, for the two roads merge again in 0.3 mile. Note the old rock work on the bed of the upper road, which is evidence of the original toll road. At 18.4 you arrive at Sphinx. The structure here is a former section house built in 1910 to serve the Park Branch of the Northern Pacific Railroad (the branch was abandoned in the 1960s, and the rails and ties were removed shortly thereafter). At 18.8 you arrive at another fork where you must bear left uphill to avoid running into a large rockfall. This stiff uphill tops out at 19.0, and you start down at 19.2 through the boulders and junipers.

At 20.1 you pass by a little farmstead situated up a canyon on your left. At 21.0, where Tom Miner Basin Road goes left, bear right onto the improved road. You pass through a picturesque settlement containing a solid-rock house which proudly states in carved numbers the year it was built, "1909." At 21.2 cross a creek and bear right.

At 21.7 you come to a junction at which a sign points right to Gardiner and Livingston. If you turn right, you'll hit the highway in about 0.3 mile. To do the complete ride, continue straight rather than turning toward the highway. At 22.1 cross Rock Creek. You're out of the timber now, riding through flat, sweeping grasslands surrounded by grand blue mountains.

At 24.8 you begin an uphill and at 25.5 top out on Point of Rocks. Begin descending at 25.9, and bottom out at the junction with US Highway 89 at 26.4 miles. If you haven't arranged for a shuttle from this point, you could turn this into a very long ride and pedal back to Mammoth on the highway, bringing the total distance to about 50 miles.

2 Divide Ride Loop

Riding surface:	pavement to primitive jeep trail
Beginning elevation:	6475 feet
Highest elevation:	8020 feet
Distance:	24.0 miles
Relative difficulty:	hard
Time to allow:	4 to 6 hours
Best time of year:	June through September
Best time of week:	any day
Supplemental maps:	Targhee National Forest Visitors Map, Targhee National Forest Travel Plan Map (Island Park District)

(Note: This loop is also on the Gallatin National Forest Visitors Map used for Ride 1 in this chapter.)

Begin riding at the junction of State Highway 87 and Forest Road 55. This junction is 18 miles west of the West Entrance to Yellowstone National Park and the town of West Yellowstone, Montana. The ride winds back and forth between the east and west sides of the Continental Divide, which forms the boundary line for the Targhee and Beaverhead national forests, as well as for the states of Idaho and Montana. You may

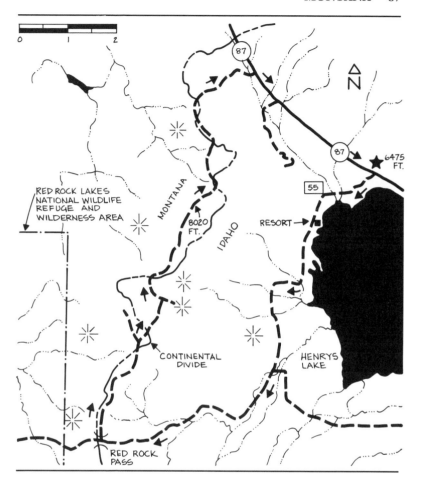

become disoriented if you pay too much attention to the signs on the divide, for the thumb of Idaho which juts into Montana at this point results in an odd alignment: Idaho, which is typically west of Montana, is actually *east* of Montana here. You'll get the picture if you study the maps beforehand.

From the junction, ride southwest gradually downhill on FR 55. There may be some traffic along the first couple miles of this smooth, dusty road, due to the busy resort you pass at 2 miles. The riding remains quite level along this well-graded road as you skirt the north and west shores of Henrys Lake. You roll through some nice aspen groves; if you have binoculars along, stop often to scan the wetlands around the shore of the lake — numerous species of migratory waterfowl nest in the area.

Route-finding on the Divide Ride Loop (Photo by Nancy McCoy)

At 9.0 miles begin a fairly steep climb which tops out a mile later at Red Rock Pass. At the pass, at 10.0, turn right onto the unsigned jeep trail, which is immediately past the sign "Red Rock Pass—7056 feet." Begin a long, mostly uphill stretch of 3 miles. Although you're getting quite high in elevation, you never do get into heavy stands of timber. Rather, the Continental Divide here passes through open sage slopes, with scatterings of timber off to the sides.

At 13.2 miles turn right, following an arrow which indicates that this trail is open to motor vehicles. The path you're turning onto is much more primitive than the road you've been on up to this point. After passing by a cattle-watering spring, begin a steep, "pusher" of an uphill. Once atop the ridge, at 13.8, you can look over the edge, down onto blue Henrys Lake and to where you were riding earlier. You'll also be rewarded with good views of Red Rock Lakes National Wildlife Refuge and Wilderness Area, and the Centennial Mountains, both to the west. Established as a refuge in 1935, Red Rock Lakes is one of the most important nesting and wintering areas in North America for the rare trumpeter swan. Other part-time and permanent residents here include bald and golden eagles, sandhill cranes, white pelicans, avocets, long-billed curlews, great blue herons, and 23 types of ducks and geese, along with over 200 other species of birds. Moose live on the refuge year-round, and deer and elk summer in the area.

Due to low use and the thick grass cover on the ridgetop, the trail becomes quite indistinct. You want to turn left, following the ridge northward, along the faded path. Even if you think you're getting off-track in this area, just aim high and follow the ridge northward, and you'll be okay. At 14.4 you turn right and pass through a gate in a barbed-wire fence.

At 14.5 pass through a log gate, and at 15.0 miles, at a T at the bottom of a steep hill, turn left and head uphill. At 15.3 you cross through a fence and re-enter Montana. At 15.6 miles, pass a second cattle-watering spring.

At 16.2 you hit a high point on the ridge and start down. Pass through a gate at 16.3. Be wary of the deep ruts in this road, and keep your pedal crank arms perpendicular to the ground. You enter some aspen and fir stands at about 17.2, and the downhill becomes quite radical as you continue down through the timber. At 20.6 miles turn right onto Hwy. 87 and ride the 3.4 miles of pavement back to your point of origin, at 24.0.

3 Grassy Lake Point to Point

Riding surface:	generally smooth gravel
Beginning elevation:	6850 feet
Highest elevation:	7319 feet
Distance:	variable
Relative difficulty:	easy
Time to allow:	1 to 6 hours
Best time of year:	June through September
Best time of week:	weekdays
Supplemental maps:	Bridger-Teton National Forest Visitors Map, Bridger-Teton National Forest Travel Plan Map (Teton Division); Targhee National Forest Visitors Map, Targhee National Forest Travel Plan Map (Ashton District)

You can make this ride as long as you want — from an easy 4- or 5-mile after-dinner spin, to an all-day or overnight journey of 60 miles plus. Or, it can be done as a 39.4-mile point to point if you arrange for a shuttle. The eastern reaches of the route pass through the John D. Rockefeller, Jr., Memorial Parkway, which fills the gap between Yellowstone and Grand Teton national parks. The western portion of the road occupies a very narrow corridor — less than 0.5 mile wide at some points — between the Jedediah Smith and Winegar Hole wilderness areas.

One particularly attractive feature of this ride is that, during the first few miles, you pass by several camping units which are a relative secret. There's a good chance you can get a site here when the campgrounds in

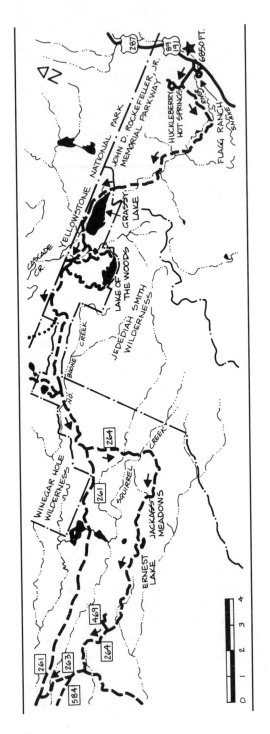

N

287
89
191
6850 FT.

HUCKLEBERRY HOT SPRINGS

FLAGG RANCH

SNAKE

JOHN D. ROCKEFELLER, JR. MEMORIAL PARKWAY

YELLOWSTONE NATIONAL PARK

GRASSY LAKE

CASCADE CR.

LAKE OF THE WOODS

JEDEDIAH SMITH WILDERNESS

NO. BOONE CREEK

264

261

SQUIRREL CREEK

JACKASS MEADOWS

WINEGAR HOLE WILDERNESS

ERNEST LAKE

469

261

263

264

584

0 1 2 3 4

70

Yellowstone and Grand Teton national parks are full. And an easy ride to one of these camping units for an overnight makes a good shakedown ride to find if you're prepared for a longer, more remote camping trip.

If you ride farther west than the turn to Lake of the Woods (at mile 13.1), you'll need the Targhee National Forest Visitors Map and the Ashton District Travel Plan Map. The Ashton District Travel Plan Map is especially important if you want to explore any of the roads or motorcycle trails which take off from the main road, because the older (pre-1985) Visitors Maps do not indicate the two, relatively new wilderness areas, Jedediah Smith and Winegar Hole, which are off-limits to bicycles.

Begin this ride 2 miles south of the South Entrance to Yellowstone Park, at the junction of US Highway 89/287/191 and the paved road which goes to Flagg Ranch, a large commercial campground. Ride west toward Flagg Ranch, and at 0.5 turn right onto Flagg-Ashton Road. At 1.1 you pass by the entrance to Huckleberry Hot Springs, which is 0.5 mile off the road. This former commercially operated springs has been razed by the NPS, and its future is uncertain at this time. In 1987, it was not closed to soaking, but signs warned swimmers to avoid getting their heads wet so as not to risk contracting amoebic meningitis. There are a number of natural pools along the creek which may be safe for soaking.

At 1.3 miles you ride onto gravel and at 1.5 pass by Camping Unit 1, which has four nice sites, situated along the green banks of the serpentine Snake River. At 2.0 you ride by Unit 2, which has one site. The riding is level through open meadows along the river's floodplain. At 2.7, near Unit 3 (two sites), you veer away from the river and begin riding in more undulating terrain.

Pass by Unit 4 at 2.9 miles and Unit 5 at 3.5. At 5.4, after a 0.2-mile downhill, you pass by Unit 6. Pass by the final two camping units — 7 and 8 — at 6.9 and 7.4 miles, respectively.

At 9.0 you leave the Rockefeller Parkway and enter the Targhee National Forest. After some stiff climbing, you crest the divide at 10.4 and begin the 0.5-mile descent to Grassy Lake Reservoir. At 11.0 miles, just prior to crossing the reservoir's dam, the road brushes up against Yellowstone Park; climb steeply away from the reservoir.

At 11.8 pass by the road which goes left to Tillery Lake, and at 12.6, cross Cascade Creek, which flows into Yellowstone Park near this point. At 13.1 pass by the turnoff to Camp Loll (Boy Scouts of America), which is 2 miles to the left, on Lake of the Woods. At 14.5 you crest Calf Creek Hill, which is followed by a 0.2-mile downhill. After a 0.5-mile level section, at the junction with South Boundary Trail, you begin a 0.5-mile

Huckleberry Hot Springs, an inviting spot for a soak on the Grassy Lake Point to Point

ascent through a very rocky area. At 15.7 you top out and start a mile-long descent down a rough stretch of road.

At 18.8 miles cross North Boone Creek; at 21.7, after riding through Gibson Meadows, you turn left onto FR 264 toward Jackass Meadows. At 23.5 pass by South Boone Creek Trail and at 24.4 you cross Squirrel Creek. At 25.1 you pass Hominy Peak Trail and start riding past a series of new, numbered logging roads. At 27.5 you ride through Jackass Meadows, and at 28.4, there's a view of the distant Teton peaks on your left.

At 29.7 you pass through an area where the USFS is encouraging the public to cut aspen for firewood, in order to stimulate the growth of new "suckers." At 29.8 lily pad–covered Ernest Lake is on your left. At 30.7 you ride by a large blow-down of aspen and conifers.

Glance behind to your left often for occasional peeks at the Tetons. The terrain is moderate, with many pleasant stands of aspen and pine.

At 33.8 miles FR 469 meets FR 264. Continue on 264 and begin a 0.5-mile downhill. The next 2 miles are through flat meadow, and at 36.6 you turn right at the T onto FR 263. At 37.2 continue straight on FR 263 (FR 584 goes left). At 37.9, after a gradual uphill, you begin a mile-long downhill to the crossing of Squirrel Creek, which you subsequently pay for with a 0.5-mile uphill to the junction with FR 261, at 39.4 miles. End (or begin) your ride here. FR 261 exits the Targhee National Forest just west of here, and the 15 miles into Ashton are flat and, due to traffic, potentially quite dusty.

4 Lulu Loop

Riding surface: smooth pavement to extremely rocky jeep
                        trail
Beginning elevation: 7600 feet
Highest elevation: 9718 feet
Distance: 14.0 miles
Relative difficulty: hard
Time to allow: 3 to 5 hours
Best time of year: July through September
Best time of week: any day
Supplemental map: Custer National Forest Visitors Map (Bear-
                        tooth Division)

If you think a 14-mile loop on which you gain, then lose, more than 2000 feet in elevation sounds like a hard ride, you're right. This is also a ride with marked contrasts — it offers you dramatic views of the unspoiled, high Beartooth Mountains, close-ups of the results of the fires that raged through the area in 1988, and encounters with deep scars and brown gashes in the mountains resulting from past and current mining activities.

The majority of this ride takes place in the Gallatin National Forest, but it also crosses into the Custer National Forest. While the Gallatin

The view near Cooke City, Montana

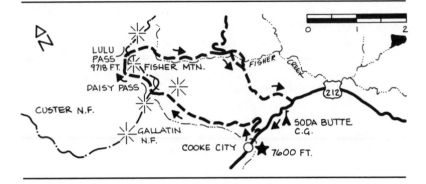

Visitors Map (detailed under the Yankee Jim Point to Point) will suffice, the roads you'll be using are depicted along the bottom edge of the map. You'll get a better overview of the surrounding country by obtaining the Custer National Forest Visitors Map (Beartooth Division).

Before getting to the Lulu Loop, there's another ride in the Beartooths worth mentioning. It is not included as a regular listing because it is a difficult ride logistically. The end is a good 80 road miles away from where you begin, although the ride itself is only about 25 miles in length.

The Morrison Jeep Trail begins high on the spectacular Beartooth Plateau, between Cooke City and Red Lodge, Montana. Starting near Long Lake, at 9655 feet, the trail climbs to about 10,150 feet before beginning its radical plunge into the Clarks Fork Canyon, where it comes in alongside the river at 4650 feet. This is a drop of 5500 feet in less than 20 miles! You definitely do *not* want to turn around and ride back to your car after this one. If you can manage to arrange for a vehicle shuttle, this adventure should not be missed. Even if you don't manage to find a way to accomplish the entire ride, just a short out and back on the Morrison Jeep Trail makes a good ride. The "on top of the world" sensation you'll experience here — combined with the reduced oxygen available at these high elevations — gives this ride a mystical quality.

The Lulu Loop begins in Cooke City, which is 4 miles east of Yellowstone National Park's Northeast Entrance. This little tourist town received national attention during the forest fires of 1988, when it had to be evacuated but was ultimately spared. Originally known as Shoofly, the town popped up along the banks of Soda Butte Creek in the 1870s. The makeshift camp eventually attracted all the businesses and vices associated with boom towns, and the hard rock mining attracted the capital of a rich easterner, Jay Cooke, Jr. Although financial troubles ultimately caused Cooke to withdraw his support, his name lives on in the town, which was renamed Cooke City.

From Cooke City, begin climbing to the east on US Highway 212. At 0.9 mile, turn left toward Daisy Pass and *really* begin climbing. This is an extremely steep grade that will grind you down. At 4.6 miles, crest Daisy Pass, at 9712 feet. In the last 3.7 miles, since turning off the pavement, you have gained just under 2000 feet in elevation, so you have an excuse for being tired! Things level out somewhat at this point, as you ride around the north end of Fisher Mountain, where you hit 9718-foot Lulu Pass at 5.9 miles. The wide vistas into the Beartooth Wilderness to the north are superb. Here you bear right and "wrap around" the back of Fisher Mountain, heading down a "wall" on switchbacks over an extremely bumpy, rocky surface. At 6.9 miles you roll through a fascinating old mining settlement.

At 8.4 miles you come alongside Fisher Creek, which is surrounded by growths of willow. At 9.1 you pass by the jeep trail which goes to Mud Lake on your left. At the fork just beyond here, bear left (although bearing right will eventually lead you to the same spot). At 9.4 pass by a cabin, and at 9.8 ride through Fisher Creek. The road condition improves once you're across the creek.

Begin a steeper downhill section at 10.0, with good views of the high Absaroka Range directly in front. At 11.8 miles, after an "invigorating" downhill, you turn right, back onto US 212 and ride past Soda Butte Campground. Continue downhill back to Cooke City, at 14.0.

4

Jackson Hole

Just to the south of Yellowstone National Park lies the wonderland known as Jackson Hole. It could be considered as part of "Yellowstone Country" except that its attractions are so outstanding and famous in their own right. This valley is about 50 miles long, north to south, and ranges from 6 to 8 miles in width. Completely surrounded by mountains, it is bounded on the east by the Gros Ventre (pronounced *grow vont*) Mountains, on the south by the Snake River and Hoback ranges, on the north by the Absarokas, and on the west by the magnificent Tetons.

Les Trois Tetons (the three breasts) were named, perhaps in a fit of hormonally induced homesickness, by early nineteenth-century French trappers. These gargantuan peaks, which erupt straight out of the valley floor, are actually a section of the earth's crust, uplifted along a fault.

With the Teton Range as a backdrop, Jackson Hole offers some of the best mountain biking to be found in the West.

The view along the RKO Loop: the spectacular Tetons rising above Jackson Hole.

Much like Sun Valley (see Chapter 5), Jackson Hole has become mountain bike crazy. Several shops in the area rent mountain bikes, and they all can recommend good rides in addition to those featured here.

A few spots favored by the mountain-biking locals are the Cache Creek–Game Creek loop, just southeast of the town of Jackson; the Gros Ventre River Road, east of the town of Kelly; and the old pass road on Teton Pass. If you want the thrill of a good downhill without having to work up a sweat to earn it, you can sign up with a local touring company that will take you and your bike to the top of Snow King Mountain Ski Area, from where you can ride the roads down the back side into Leeks Canyon, to US Highway 191.

The supplemental maps listed for each ride in this chapter are available from Bridger-Teton National Forest Supervisor's Office, 340 North Cache St., Jackson, WY 83001, (307) 733-2752.

1 RKO Loop

Riding surface:	pavement to extremely rocky and bumpy
Beginning elevation:	6680 feet
Highest elevation:	6945 feet
Lowest elevation:	6555 feet
Distance:	27.5 miles
Relative difficulty:	easy
Time to allow:	3 to 5 hours
Best time of year:	May through October
Best time of week:	any day
Supplemental maps:	Bridger-Teton National Forest Visitors Map (Jackson and Buffalo ranger districts), Bridger-Teton National Forest Travel Plan Map (Teton Division)

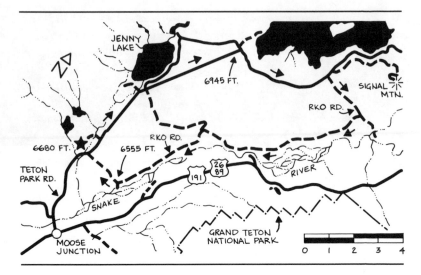

The RKO Loop is entirely within Grand Teton National Park on paved or primitive roads. Whether you should ride the paved stretch first or last depends upon what time of day you're heading out. The primitive RKO Road passes through superb wildlife-viewing areas; there are opportunities to see bison, elk, moose, and deer, as well as many types of smaller mammals and birds along the river. To enhance your chances of spotting animals, you should ride this stretch during the first light or the last light of day. Therefore, if you're doing the ride in the morning, ride the RKO Road first; if you're riding in the evening, do the paved section first. In addition to optimizing your chances of seeing animals, you'll avoid the wide-open sage flats during the middle of the day — it can get downright hot out there, even at such a high altitude.

This is a good ride for a day when the weather is less than favorable, for it won't be as nasty here as in the higher country, although it can get windy out in the open. This also would make a fantastic full-moon ride!

The evening ride: At Moose Junction, 12 miles north of Jackson on U.S. Highway 191/89/26, turn into Grand Teton National Park on Teton Park Road. Begin your riding 4 miles north of here, where RKO Rd. meets Teton Park Rd. Ride north on the paved Teton Park Rd. The riding is quite level along here, although you do gain a couple hundred feet during the next 6 miles, and it provides you with tremendous views of the high Teton peaks. At 3.5 miles the turnoff to sparkling Jenny Lake is on your left.

Just before curving right at mile 7.6, you crest the ride's high point.

At 12.0 miles, after curving around the south end of Jackson Lake, turn right onto RKO Road (if you come to the turnoff to Signal Mountain, you've gone 0.3 mile too far). Ride eastward on this primitive, rocky road, and at 14.1 turn right up the hill (the road going straight dead-ends down by the Snake River). The terrain becomes gently undulating. The primitive and bumpy nature of this road, combined with the fact that the NPS doesn't go out of its way to promote it, precludes all but extremely adventurous motorists.

At 15.4 bear right on the main track. At 18.5 go left at the fork (although you'll be okay if you go right, since the two trails merge once again in 0.7 mile) and ride along the edge of the cliff above the Snake River. This primary tributary of the Columbia River has also been known as the Lewis, Mad Shoshone, Saptin, Nez Perce, and Sagebrush, among other names. How it became known as the Snake, no one knows for certain. The name may stem from the serpentine course the river cuts through the open plateau, or from the Indians which lived along its banks. Regardless of the current name and its derivation, this is as pretty a river in as gorgeous a setting as exists anywhere in the world.

Keep a lookout for bald eagles and ospreys, and their nests. The Snake River is one of the endangered bald eagle's primary nesting locations in the greater Yellowstone ecosystem, which is, in turn, one of the only healthy nesting areas in the Rocky Mountains. More than 60 pairs of the eagles nest permanently in the region, and as many as 300 live in the area during winter.

At 20.4 miles you encounter a steep uphill with loose river cobbles; you'll probably have to walk part of this. The uphill takes you onto the next terrace above the floodplain. The Grand Teton rises sharply in front of you, remarkable in its sheer magnitude and the attention it commands. As the sun sets on the Tetons' far side, the day's last rays of light filter through the deeper valleys, setting the table for a visual feast.

At 21.5 miles you pass by a road on your right which is blocked off, and then you ride straight down the middle of a dry wash, onto the second terrace above the river — watch out, the river cobbles create tricky steering conditions. Near 22.5 you're afforded good views of the Gros Ventre Slide, off in the distance about 9 miles to your left. In 1925 the top of this slope broke loose 2000 feet above the Gros Ventre River. Earth, rocks, and trees roared down the mountainside and across the river valley, and rubble carried 400 feet up the opposite slope. The debris, more than 200 feet deep and a mile across, blocked the river, which resulted in the formation of 5-mile-long Lower Slide Lake. Two years later this natural dam failed; the ensuing flood wiped out the original town of Kelly.

At 22.9 miles you arrive at another good viewpoint above the Snake, and yet another at 24.0. At 26.0, near the entrance to the private BarBC Ranch, bear right, away from the river. At 27.5 you return to the beginning point.

2 Blackrock Loop

Riding surface:	pavement to somewhat bumpy gravel
Beginning elevation:	6880 feet
Highest elevation:	8640 feet
Lowest elevation:	6797 feet
Distance:	28.8 miles or 41.8 miles
Relative difficulty:	moderate
Time to allow:	3 to 7 hours
Best time of year:	June through September
Best time of week:	any day
Supplemental maps:	Bridger-Teton National Forest Visitors Map (Jackson and Buffalo ranger districts), Bridger-Teton National Forest Travel Plan Map (Teton Division)

The shorter, 28.8 mile, option for this ride contains about 6 miles of pavement riding; the 41.8-mile loop includes 15.5 miles of pavement, 10 of those on the very quiet, low-traffic Buffalo Fork Road. If you have the time and energy, try the longer of the two.

The ride begins at Hatchet Campground, which is immediately west of Blackrock Ranger Station on Forest Road 30160 (designated FR 014 on the USFS maps). The ranger station is 8 miles east of Moran Junction on US Highway 26/287. From the campground, ride west on this gravel road, noting the sign warning you that this is grizzly country (somehow, such signs are hard to miss!). Start riding uphill immediately on this wide, well-graded road.

At 2.0, as you rise above the valley floor, you meet superb views of the distant Teton peaks. At 3.6 miles ride past a beaver pond and continue on the similar-surfaced road (a lower-quality road goes left, through a gate). At 4.3 you pass a sign pointing toward the "Diamond L Ranch— 3 mi." At 4.6 you begin a downhill. At this point a double-track jeep path departs from the main road — you'll note several of these throughout this ride, enticing you to explore off-route.

At 5.6 miles bear left toward Lily Lake, continuing on FR 30160, and begin an uphill. The views of the Tetons over Sagebrush Flat demand

A view along the Blackrock Loop

that you stop and take some pictures. A trail, off to the right, begins paralleling the road at this point. Switchback to the right at 6.8, and arrive at Lily Lake at 8.3 miles.

A sign here reads, "Trumpeter Swan Nesting Area — to provide security during the critical nesting period, the area within a $\frac{1}{4}$- mile radius of Lily Lake has been closed. Any human presence may disturb nesting swans." The rare trumpeter swan is the largest of all North American waterfowl.

The USFS is working at securing and enhancing swan habitat through a program called SWAN ACTION. Because the trumpeters tend to be very sensitive to human disturbance, the USFS has instituted land-management practices in swan habitat such as leaving or creating buffer strips of cover, closing roads, and timing resource activities so they're less apt to disturb the swans.

The pleasant park through which you're riding is surrounded by aspen-covered slopes and open meadows. At 8.8 miles go straight rather than bearing right; the road surface becomes very smooth. At 10.8 miles crest a hill, and at 11.2 you cross a bridge. At 11.6 bear left on Flagstaff Road (here a sign reads "Hwy. 287—6 mi."). At this point you begin paralleling Flagstaff Creek upstream. The riding is generally uphill, but there are a couple of level stretches which provide relief. Top out on a divide at 15.1 miles and begin a long section of rolling hills.

At 18.0 cross Blackrock Creek and arrive at US 26/287 at 18.4 miles. Turn left onto this potentially busy highway, which happens to be a portion of the TransAmerica Bicycle Trail. Developed in 1975 by Bikecentennial in association with America's Bicentennial celebration, this 4500-mile network of back roads links Astoria, Oregon, and Williamsburg, Virginia. Don't be surprised if you come across some loaded-

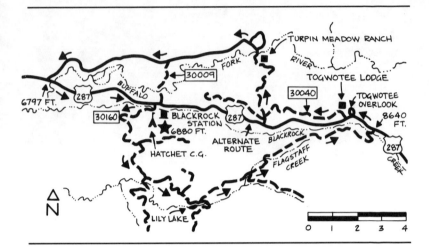

down cross-country cyclists on this stretch of road, because several hundred people ride across the United States on the route every year.

At 19.3 pass by the Togwotee (pronounced *TOE-guhty*) Overlook, and at 19.5 turn right into the Togwotee Lodge parking area. Ride on the road which goes between the left (west) end of the lodge building and the adjacent cabins. Pass through a gate onto the road signed, "FR 30040" (designated FR 011 on the USFS maps). At 20.0 continue straight across a cattle guard (another path goes right). The road you're riding on is a primitive double-track trail that probably becomes very sloppy when wet. This is a damper, more shaded slope than where you were previously riding, and the wildflowers in middle and late summer are wonderful.

At 22.8 bear left on the similar-surfaced road and pass through another gate at 23.1. At 23.5 miles you arrive at a T. If you want to do the shorter loop, turn left onto this high-quality gravel road and ride the 0.3 mile to US Highway 287/26, onto which you turn right, and return to the beginning point at 28.8 miles. To accomplish the longer loop, turn right onto this road and begin a fun, smooth 3.7-mile downhill.

At 27.2, at the bottom of the downhill, pass through the Turpin Meadow Ranch, which is a working dude ranch. At 27.4 cross the Buffalo Fork River and begin a paved, rolling ride through the pleasant river valley. At 31.3, at the top of a hill, FR 30009 takes off to your left (it's designated FR 009 on the USFS maps).

At 37.1 you arrive back at US 287, onto which you turn left. After 4.7 miles of highway riding, you're back at Hatchet Campground at 41.8 miles.

3 Monument Ridge Loop

Riding surface: pavement to very bumpy
Beginning elevation: 6380 feet
Highest elevation: 8257 feet
Distance: 22.0 or 27.0 miles
Relative difficulty: hard
Time to allow: 3 to 5 hours
Best time of year: June through September
Best time of week: any day
Supplemental maps: Bridger-Teton National Forest Visitors Map
                            (Jackson and Buffalo ranger districts),
                            Bridger-Teton National Forest Travel Plan
                            Map (Teton Division)

Begin this ride at the junction of US Highway 189/191 and Cliff Creek Road (Forest Road 046), which is 15 miles southeast of Hoback Junction, or 6 miles northwest of the town of Bondurant. Kozy Campground (USFS) is 1.5 miles northwest of your beginning point.

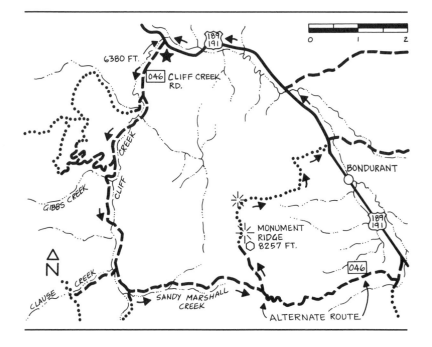

Aspen "highway sign," Monument Ridge Loop

Ride south on the gravel road, following Cliff Creek upstream. It's a smooth road, and the uphill grade is gentle. At 1.5 miles you start catching glimpses of the red ridges of the Hoback Range as you ride alongside the meandering, sparkling stream.

At 3.4 miles, where a road goes uphill to the right, bear left. At 3.9 miles cross Gibbs Creek after a fun little downhill. At 5.2 you cross Cliff Creek and meander through wildflower-filled meadows. At 6.4 miles pass by a closed road to the right, which goes up Clause Creek. At 7.0 bear left, leaving Cliff Creek, and head up the Sandy Marshall Creek drainage. As you progress along this road, the grade steepens and the road surface becomes very bumpy. This surface would likely get very mucky in a rainstorm (unlike the first 7 miles of the ride, which are along a well-drained surface).

At 8.6 miles you cross a cattle guard, after which the road surface becomes quite rutted. It gets very steep and rough, up to 10.7 miles, where you pass through a gate. Continue uphill for another 0.1 mile, and then turn left up the ridge onto an unsigned, primitive road (this path

84

continues downhill, to the right, as well). As you commence climbing up the ridge, you're rewarded with views of the Wind River Range to your right.

The climb becomes quite steep. The terrain is mostly open, with occasional stands of timber. You arrive at the old lookout cabin at the top of Monument Ridge at 12.5 miles. The 360-degree panorama on top makes all the climbing you've done more than worth the trouble! You can see the Wind River, Hoback, and Gros Ventre ranges, and if you look closely to the north, just the very tip of what must be the Grand Teton. If you peer down over the edge to the east, you'll see a series of beaver ponds stair-stepped down the drainage.

Once you've soaked up all the views, if you want to return the easier, but longer, way, ride back down the ridge to where you turned left onto the primitive road (at 10.8 miles), and turn left here at 14.2. Head *steeply* down into Clark Draw, and arrive at US 189/191 at about 18.5 miles. Here you turn left onto the highway and return to the junction with Cliff Creek Rd. at 27.0.

However, if you want to do the more difficult trail ride, continue up-ridge (north) from the cabin. After cresting two small knolls, you arrive at a ditch, which you cross. Begin riding downhill on the trail, which follows a ridge into a timber stand. At 13.3, just when you thought it was all downhill from here, you have a steep 0.2-mile uphill. At 13.5 resume riding downhill on the trail, which becomes less distinct, almost vague in places. You'll occasionally need to heft your bicycle over the ample downfall covering the trail, and in some areas, the trail is very bumpy.

At 14.4 another, quite worn-looking trail crosses the one you're on. Continue straight. Near this point you'll see a blaze carved in an aspen, along with someone's clever knife work which reads "US 101" within a US highway symbol–shaped shield.

As you approach 15.1 miles, the trail becomes markedly more distinct, and yet another trail crosses yours. Ride through a gate and onto an open slope which contains some huge sage "trees." Here you'll gain a true appreciation for what it means to be a "rider of the purple sage"!

At 16.4, as you approach US 189/191, turn left across the draw and follow the fence line for 0.1 mile, and then turn left onto the pavement. After 5.5 miles of highway riding, you return to the beginning point at 22.0 miles. If you're sore and jolted after this strenuous ride, make like a racehorse and immerse your tired legs in the icy waters of Cliff Creek. It'll work wonders.

5

Sun Valley and the Sawtooth National Recreation Area

Pedal east from Sun Valley up Trail Creek on a sunny rainbow September morning, and you'll appreciate the words inscribed on Ernest Hemingway's memorial, which is tucked away in a grove alongside the creek:

> Best of all he loved the fall
> The leaves yellow on the cottonwoods
> Leaves floating on the trout streams
> And above the hills
>   the high blue windless skies
> Now he will be part of them forever

More than at any other area in this guide, Idaho's famous playground, Sun Valley, has become an established center for mountain-biking. Most of the bike shops in Sun Valley and the nearby town of Ketchum rent mountain bikes, and most of the best rides in the area are already described in a guidebook (see Appendix B) and a USFS brochure. For that reason, this chapter includes only one ride in the immediate Sun Valley area, the Adams Gulch Loop, as a sample of the fine mountain-biking available. Beginning and ending in downtown Ketchum, this loop is the most popular ride in the area. The remainder of the rides in this chapter are in the nearby Sawtooth National Recreation Area (SNRA). This area offers riding as good as that around Sun Valley, but it is often ignored by visitors in a rush to get to "rich and famous" Sun Valley.

The primary focus here is on easy and moderate rides within the SNRA. Rides 4 through 7 are short out and backs based out of USFS campgrounds in the area. The elevation gained/lost on all of them is minimal, making them ideal as after-supper "digestion aids." Before heading out, be sure and stop by the SNRA Visitor Center, which is 8 miles north of Ketchum. They have set up some nice displays, and they sell a number of interesting books on the history and natural history of the area.

There are two commercial ski-touring centers here whose trails provide fun mountain-biking during the warmer months. Galena Lodge, at the southern foot of Galena Pass, is 23 miles north of Ketchum. Galena's trails are on USFS land, so the public is free to use them at no cost. Busterback Ranch is 20 miles south of Stanley, or 40 miles north of Ketchum. At this writing, the ranch was just beginning to promote mountain biking.

In August 1972 Congress enacted legislation which created the SNRA. Portions of four mountain ranges — the Smokies, the Boulders, the White Clouds, and the crown-jewel Sawtooths — lie inside the 754,000-acre recreation area. Within the SNRA, the Sawtooth Wilderness contains 216,000 acres, and portions of the White Clouds will soon be designated as wilderness as well. The Salmon, the famed "River of No Return," is born in the high country of the SNRA, and within the boundaries of this outdoors paradise lie no fewer than 300 high-mountain lakes.

The supplemental maps you'll want to carry for the SNRA are available from Sawtooth National Recreation Area, Headquarters Office, Star Route, Hwy. 75, Ketchum, ID 83340, (208) 726-8291.

1 Adams Gulch Loop

Riding surface:	smooth dirt jeep road or trail with many stream crossings
Beginning elevation:	5880 feet
Highest elevation:	7720 feet
Distance:	12.9 or 14.5 miles
Relative difficulty:	out and back on Adams Gulch Road — easy; entire loop — hard
Time to allow:	2 to 5 hours
Best time of year:	June through October
Best time of week:	weekdays
Supplemental maps:	Sawtooth National Forest Visitors Map (north half), Sawtooth National Forest Travel Plan Map

This ride is the only one in this chapter which is not within the Sawtooth National Recreation Area. However, it is in the Sawtooth National Forest (Ketchum District). Motorized vehicles are not permitted on the trails in Adams Gulch (they *are* allowed on the Adams Gulch Road), but the USFS encourages mountain biking on the area's trails.

Riding up the bridle trails, Adams Gulch Loop

Beginning at the junction of Main Street and Warm Springs Road in Ketchum, ride west on Warm Springs Rd. In 0.5 mile, cross the Big Wood River. At 1.3 miles, just past the Heidelberg Inn, turn right onto Wanderer Street. In another 0.1 mile, at the end of this street, ride through a horse corral area onto a bridle path which climbs straight ahead. This is a quite steep, exposed ascent into a sage-filled draw.

There's a good chance you'll run into some equestrians on this part of the ride. If approaching from the rear, call out so the riders know you're coming. As mentioned in the introduction to this guide, it's a good policy to dismount and walk your bike when overtaking a horse (whether from the front or the rear), both for the safety of yourself and the horse and rider.

At 2.2 miles, crest the saddle and start down into a shaded, north-facing draw. At 2.3, rather than continuing on the main path, bear left onto a lesser-quality trail through the woods. At 2.5 bear straight through the woods, and in about 50 yards, turn right. This brings you down to the Adams Gulch Rd., onto which you turn left. This jeep road is gradually uphill and very smooth. It's open to vehicles, but few use it. You have an open sage hillside on your right and forest on your left.

At 3.1 miles you encounter the first of many stream crossings. These are fun and quite easy to manage, but you do want to steer clear of the larger cobbles. At 3.8 miles you have another stream crossing, another at 4.0, and yet another at 4.1. Pass Trail 146, which goes left up the West

Fork of Eve Gulch at 4.3 miles and continue up Adams Gulch Trail 177, which is still a jeep road at this point.

You have three more stream crossings at 4.4, 4.6, and 4.7 miles. After the third of these you'll be on the right (north) side of the creek. Note the stone cairn on your right (you'll be turning here on your way down if you do the complete loop). Continue up the road.

At 5.2 miles is stream crossing number eight. After crossing, bear right on the trail, rather than following the road up into the woods. At 5.8 miles you come to a spot where the trail again crosses the stream. It's best to turn around here, as beyond this point the riding becomes less enjoyable. At 6.9 miles you're back at the cairn. If you want to complete the loop, turn sharp left here, onto the trail. If you prefer not to get into the tough stuff, just continue out the way you came in and pick up the narrative at mile 10.7. Total mileage for this ride is 12.9.

For those riding the entire loop, you begin a stiff climb into a draw. The trail crosses back and forth from side to side of the little creek. From 7.8 to 8.5 you'll be forced to dismount occasionally and walk up steep and rocky sections of the trail. At 8.5 you arrive at a saddle with a big rocky point to your left and an opening which slopes gently uphill on your right. The views are worth relishing!

In another 0.1 mile, you have a short walker out of a draw, after which you commence sidehill riding. At 9.1 crest a high point on the side of a ridge and begin down. Once you're up on top and looking back into Adams Gulch, there are a number of ways to get down, but all the trails eventually lead back to the road. If you bear left at the first fork in the trail, you'll come to the back of a sign at 9.2. Continue straight on the same trail, and begin down a section of switchbacks and tricky trail riding which leads through shimmering aspen groves. Go down, down, down!

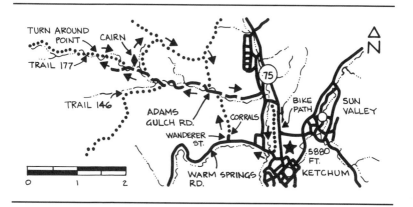

At 10.7 miles turn left back onto Adams Gulch Road and cross the stream (you may have emerged at a spot some distance from this one; still, turn left onto Adams Gulch Road). At 11.1 there's another trail coming in on the left. At 11.2 ride straight past the bridle/ski trails on which you rode into Adams Gulch. At 11.7 miles ride through a gate, leaving the Sawtooth National Forest. Pedal onto pavement in 0.1 mile, and coast past some astounding, expensive-looking homes.

At 12.2 bear right at the Y and head toward the bridge. At 12.5 miles cross the Big Wood River. At 12.7, immediately before the highway, turn right onto the paved bicycle path. Pass through several road intersections, and at 14.0, turn left onto Warm Springs Rd. At 14.5 you're back at the junction with Main St. in Ketchum.

2 Decker Flat Loop

Riding surface:	from smooth, powdery dirt to pavement
Beginning elevation:	6490 feet
Highest elevation:	6920 feet
Distance:	23.3 miles
Relative difficulty:	moderate
Time to allow:	3 to 5 hours
Best time of year:	June through October
Best time of week:	any day
Supplemental maps:	Sawtooth National Forest Visitors Map (north half), Sawtooth National Forest Travel Plan Map

Ride this loop in the early morning or late evening, the times best for spotting wildlife. The ride begins at Mountain View Campground on Little Redfish Lake. The campgrounds at this lake are very popular. If you plan to stay overnight and have no luck in finding a site, check across Highway 75 at Sunny Gulch Campground.

Redfish Lake has the only population of sockeye salmon found in Idaho, though the number that returns each year has dropped to 50 or lower. They migrate upstream during July, August, and early September. Once, no fewer than five of the seven large glacial lakes which grace the east slope of the Sawtooths supported populations of sockeye salmon. However, construction of dams on the Snake and Columbia rivers has all but eliminated the spawning run of these fish.

Pedaling through stands of lodgepole pine, Decker Flat Loop

Redfish Lake turnoff is on State Highway 75, 5 miles south of Stanley. Turn from the highway toward the lake, and arrive at the campground at 0.6 mile.

Exit the campground and turn left toward the highway. At 0.3 mile turn right onto dirt Forest Road 210, winding up through the timber onto a rocky moraine. At 0.5 bear straight ahead rather than going right.

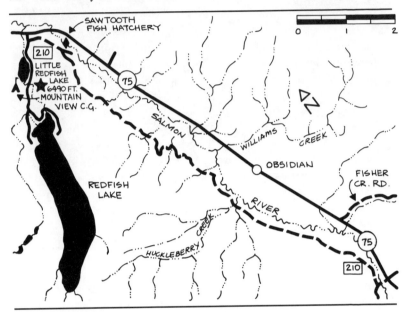

In another 0.1 mile zip down a short hill and begin up again. If the weather has been dry, the road surface will be quite powdery. This soft surface can be tricky to steer in, so use caution and spin low gears.

At 1.4 miles, at a three-way junction, bear right on signed FR 210. Beginning here, you'll encounter a series of short (0.2- to 0.8-mile) ups and downs, some quite steep and powdery, and a few stretches with large rocks embedded in the road. At 4.2 you skirt a meadow; views of the Sawtooth peaks are on your right. The road surface becomes more compacted in this vicinity. At 5.0 top out and begin a 0.5-mile downhill, after which you curve left and begin a steep uphill. Are you asking yourself yet why this is called the Decker *Flat* Loop?!

At 6.0 miles top out and begin a long downhill, passing through a stand of big Douglas fir. At 6.8 you coast out of the timber and onto the Salmon River floodplain and Decker Flat. Here you're provided with open views of the White Cloud Mountains on your left and the Smokies straight ahead. At 7.0 turn sharp right. The road becomes a level, double-track path. You're riding along the first bench above the Salmon.

At 7.5 pass a nice picnic/camping spot on your right. You begin riding directly alongside the river at this point. Cross Huckleberry Creek at 7.9 on a paved bridge, after which the road becomes wider and well-graded. You have good views of the Sawtooths behind on your right.

At 11.8, directly beside the Salmon once again, you enter a stand of timber with good camping/picnic sites. At 12.0 you arrive at a T; turn left and cross the Salmon River. At 12.3 you turn left onto Hwy. 75, which is wide and level, with a good shoulder for bicycling. You're now rewarded with constant views of the rugged Sawtooths.

At 14.0 is the junction of Hwy. 75 and Fisher Creek Road. This is the beginning point for what many consider to be the classic Sawtooth Valley ride — the Fisher Creek–Williams Creek loop. This loop was opened to mountain bikes and motorcycles in 1988, but the easternmost section may be included in a new wilderness area which will include parts of the White Cloud Range. SNRA personnel, in early 1988, thought that the road would likely be written out of the wilderness, but you'll want to stop in at SNRA headquarters to check the status of the land before riding the loop.

Continuing up Hwy. 75, at 15.9 is Sessions Lodge and a convenience store, which together make up the lion's share of the town of Obsidian. At 17.9, on your right, is the entrance to Idaho Rocky Mountain Ranch. You may want to pedal in 0.5 mile and have a look at this historic western guest ranch. At 21.2 the Sawtooth Fish Hatchery is on your left. The ongoing efforts to improve salmon and steelhead spawning conditions and rear smolts from eggs make a fascinating story, and a visit to the hatchery is worthwhile.

At 22.0 miles cross over a bridge to the west side of the Salmon. After cresting a small hill, turn left onto Redfish Lake Road at 22.7, and at 23.3 miles return to Mountain View Campground.

3 Nip and Tuck Loop

Riding surface:	mostly smooth dirt or gravel, with some big boulders on Joe's Gulch Jeep Trail
Beginning elevation:	6200 feet
Highest elevation:	7000 feet
Lowest elevation:	6170 feet
Distance:	13.8 miles
Relative difficulty:	moderate
Time to allow:	2 to 3 hours
Best time of year:	June through October
Best time of week:	any day
Supplemental maps:	Sawtooth National Forest Visitors Map (north half), Sawtooth National Forest Travel Plan Map

Steep grades and abrupt slopes typify these mountains.

Stanley is a great little cow town. Some top-notch commercial river runners headquarter out of here, so you might consider doing a Salmon River float while you're in the area. This ride begins in Lower Stanley, which is about a mile northeast of Stanley on State Highway 75 (and if you think Stanley, population 97, is small, wait until you see Lower Stanley!). The ride begins, ends, and takes place mostly within the Sawtooth National Recreation Area, but you do leave it and ride onto the Challis National Forest for part of the distance.

At 0.1 mile east of the gas stations and store in Lower Stanley, turn left (northwest) from Hwy. 75 up unsigned Nip and Tuck Creek Road. Start uphill into an arid, sage-filled draw on a very smooth road surface. At 1.2 the grade steepens, and at 1.6 miles a lesser-quality road takes off to the left; you continue straight. At 2.5 miles top out and cross a cattle guard, and enjoy the views of the Salmon River Mountains to the north. Descend into a stand of timber and continue straight at 2.8 as you pass a road veering to the left.

At 3.4 miles bottom out and begin a series of roller-coaster hills through the basin bottom. At 4.9 you arrive at a three-way junction, where you bear right onto the curving road. In 0.2 mile, immediately

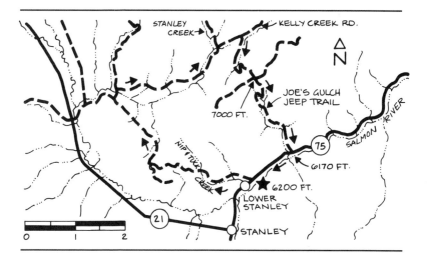

after crossing a cattle guard, turn right onto the wide gravel road signed, "Placer Diggings." You're still in the open basin, where you have wide-open views of the distant Sawtooths. At 7.0 miles you enter a narrower, timbered valley. At 7.8 bear right onto Kelly Creek Road, which is a continuation of the road surface you've been on (the lesser-quality road to the left follows Stanley Creek).

At 8.5 turn right onto Joe's Gulch Jeep Trail and begin climbing into deep woods. The road winds up and down at first and is basically smooth, with occasional ruts. At 9.2 the surface becomes very rutted as you begin a steep uphill, and at 9.5 you switchback hard left. At 9.7 there's a temporary topping out, and at 9.9 you bear right on the higher-quality road. At 10.1 you top out and pass straight through a USFS gate (there are high-quality roads going both right and left at this point which are not shown on the Visitors Map); begin a long downhill. In 0.1 mile bear right.

At 10.6 switchback hard right as you ride down a virtual wall. At 10.8 miles switchback hard left, away from an old building foundation. At 11.2 cross the drainage bottom and continue straight. This is a fun downhill, through a canyon which is reminiscent of those in the South-west. At 11.5 you wrap around the side of a cliff and then cross a draw at 11.7. At 12.2 miles pass through an open gateway; ride carefully, because you're atop a platform chiseled in the side of the wall. At 12.7 you pass under a set of high wires, and then turn right onto Hwy. 75 and begin paralleling the Salmon River. At 13.8 miles you're back at the junction with Nip and Tuck Creek Rd. in Lower Stanley.

4 Chemeketan Campground Out and Back

Riding surface:	smooth dirt to quite rocky
Beginning elevation:	7520 feet
Highest elevation:	7750 feet
Distance:	6 miles (12.5 if you begin at Galena Pass)
Relative difficulty:	easy
Time to allow:	1 to 2 hours
Best time of year:	July through October
Best time of week:	any day
Supplemental maps:	Sawtooth National Forest Visitors Map, Sawtooth National Forest Travel Plan Map

At the northern foot of Galena Pass, half-way between Ketchum and Stanley on Highway 75, turn south onto Salmon River Road, FR 215. From here to Chemeketan Campground, it is 3.1 miles, which you can drive. Alternatively, one member of your party could drive and let the others ride in, for it's a smooth, level, and pretty ride. (Note: Chemeketan is a reservations-only campground, so you should contact the Sawtooth National Recreation Area headquarters in advance if you plan to camp here.)

If you are going to do a combination of riding and driving to the campground, there's an addition which will make this a quite memorable ride (and a somewhat more challenging one than the "out and back" described here). From the Galena Summit overlook (elevation 8701 feet), go 0.2 mile northwest (toward Stanley). At this point the old pass road, which is gravel and dirt, takes off from the south side of Hwy. 75. If you start riding here, you'll have a *screamer* of a downhill (beware of erosional ditches where you cross drainages). It's 3.5 miles down to where the old pass road meets FR 215 heading into Chemeketan Campground (at a point just off Hwy. 75). It's a total of about 6.5 miles from the top of the pass to the campground.

To do the campground ride, ride south from the northern edge of Chemeketan Campground. At 0.2 mile exit from the timber and ride into a large meadow. A sign here reads, "Narrow, rough road ahead." At 0.4 you skirt the left side of the meadow as you ride on a pleasant double-track road. At 0.6 begin winding through the woods on a smooth surface, and at 0.9 you re-enter meadow. At 1.5 miles is a stretch of river cobbles, and at 1.7 you cross the Salmon River (you're near the headwaters, so the river

USFS campgrounds offer pleasant spots to base out of for several days of riding in the same area.

is quite small at this point in mid-summer). Cross it again at 2.0, and bear right. At 2.1 the road becomes rocky and you begin climbing sharply. At 3.0, where the riding is becoming very difficult anyway, the road is gated shut. Return to the campground the way you came.

There's another enticing road which takes off immediately at the north edge of the campground. From the campground, pedal to the north, and ride through a creek. This road bears right immediately after you cross the creek, and begins following it upstream. The surface is smooth at the beginning, and it might be worth exploring.

5 Stanley Lake Out and Back

Riding surface:	sandy trail with creek crossings
Beginning elevation:	6450 feet
Highest elevation:	6860 feet
Distance:	8 miles
Relative difficulty:	easy
Time to allow:	1 to 2 hours
Best time of year:	July through October
Best time of week:	weekdays
Supplemental maps:	Sawtooth National Forest Visitors Map, Sawtooth National Forest Travel Plan Map

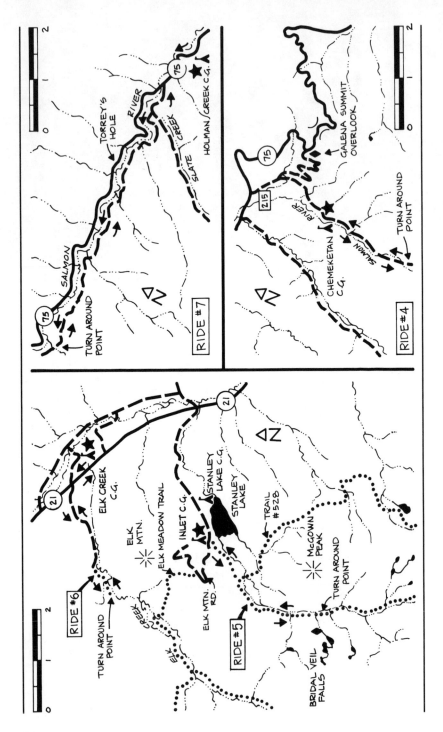

RIDE #7

2
1
0

N

75

TORREY'S HOLE

RIVER

SLATE CREEK

HOLMAN CREEK C.G.

75

SALMON

TURN AROUND POINT

RIDE #4

2
1
0

N

75

GALENA SUMMIT OVERLOOK

215

RIVER

CHEMEKETAN C.G.

SALMON

TURN AROUND POINT

RIDE #6

2
1
0

N

21

21

ELK CREEK C.G.

ELK MEADOW TRAIL

ELK MTN.

INLET C.G.

STANLEY LAKE C.G.

STANLEY LAKE

TRAIL #528

ELK MTN. RD.

ELK CREEK

McGOWN PEAK

TURN AROUND POINT

RIDE #5

TURN AROUND POINT

BRIDAL VEIL FALLS

A common campsite visitor in the SNRA

Here it is — the *perfect* trail, in a breathtaking, Sawtooth peak–surrounded setting. The turnoff to Stanley Lake is 5 miles west of the main junction in Stanley, on State Highway 21. Head to Inlet Campground, which is 3.5 miles from the highway. The trail you'll be riding on originates near Site 9 in Area B. Where you pass through a gate, the trail is signed "Alpine Way Trail, 1; Summit, 7." Pedal upstream along Stanley Lake Creek on a stretch of trail open to two-wheel travel. The sandy trail starts out level and very smooth. You gain a total of about 300 feet of elevation over the course of the next 4 miles.

At 1.0 mile bear right at the sign, toward Sawtooth Lake (Alpine Way Trail 528, which is closed to vehicles including mountain bikes, veers to the left at this point). At 1.3 you ride through sweet-scented, colorful meadow. Coast through the creek here, and again at 1.5, then hit a steep uphill section. If you find yourself spinning out in the loose sand and dirt, try this: Stand on your pedals, but don't lean out over your handlebars, because this moves your weight off the rear tire, where it's needed for traction. Instead, lean back and hang on with straightened arms — much like a water skier does.

At about 2.5 miles you have another fun creek crossing. At 4.0 you arrive at the point beyond which vehicles are not allowed. Down along the creek, which is to your right, there are some nice spots for picnicking and soaking up the sunshine. At this point you have a view of Bridal Veil Falls, high up in the peaks on the other side of the valley.

On your way back to Stanley Lake, resist the temptation to zoom down the trail. This is a popular area, and quite a few other recreationists use this trail. Also, the rocks, roots, and sporadically loose sand could set you unexpectedly airborne. For caution's sake, give out a yelp before heading around blind corners.

If you leave Inlet Campground and turn left onto FR 469, you'll arrive at the Elk Meadow Trail on your left after 1.8 miles of steep climbing. The USFS plans soon to have a distinct trail, open to motorcycles and mountain bikes, leading into Elk Meadow. Here it will join the trail along Elk Creek, which is described in the next campground ride. Details are available at the Sawtooth National Recreation Area Headquarters or at the Stanley District Ranger Station.

6 Elk Creek Out and Back

Riding surface:	pavement to gravel to trail
Beginning elevation:	6540 feet
Highest elevation:	6720 feet
Distance:	7.2 miles
Relative difficulty:	easy
Time to allow:	1 to 2 hours
Best time of year:	July through October
Best time of week:	any day
Supplemental maps:	Sawtooth National Forest Visitors Map, Sawtooth National Forest Travel Plan Map

Begin this pleasant, flat ride at Elk Creek Campground, a group/reservation campground (for information, contact the Stanley District Ranger Station at 208/774-3681). The campground is about 8.5 miles west of Stanley on State Highway 21.

Leave the campground and turn right (northwest) onto State Highway 21. At 0.6 mile, turn left onto Elk Creek Road, which is flat and well graded at this point. At 0.9 bear left toward Elk Creek (this junction is not shown on the 1985 Visitors Map). At 1.1 you're riding through a young forest of lodgepole pine; the road becomes narrow and rougher, and at 1.8 miles it becomes even more primitive.

At 2.3 miles note the old buildings off to your left. The primitive road soon becomes a trail. At 3.1, after a stretch right along the creek, you arrive at a hiker-biker registration box. You can ride along the trail quite easily for another 0.5 mile, and for another 0.5 mile past this with some difficulty, due to downfall and marshy areas, before turning back to the campground. The chances of spotting wildlife here are very good, so early morning and evening would be the perfect times for this ride. (As mentioned in the previous campground ride, soon it should be possible to tie this trail in with the Elk Meadow Trail and come out at Inlet Campground.)

7 Salmon River Canyon Out and Back

Riding surface: pavement to bumpy gravel and dirt
Beginning elevation: 5620 feet
Highest elevation: 6000 feet
Distance: 16 miles
Relative difficulty: easy
Time to allow: 2 to 4 hours
Best time of year: June through October
Best time of week: any day
Supplemental maps: Sawtooth National Forest Visitors Map,
                        Sawtooth National Forest Travel Plan Map

As you drive east from Stanley on State Highway 75, the Salmon River rolls, tumbles, and froths beside you. Out of the high country, through the timber, down the canyon, and into the desert you travel together. At 11 miles east of Stanley is Sunbeam Hot Springs, a primitive, non-commercial springs where someone graciously has constructed a large, stone changing-room. These fuming hot pools just below the highway are flush with the Salmon. You'll have to plug some holes with river cobbles or fill in some cracks with sand to get *your* pool just right. Once it's perfect you can relax and melt, eye-level with but isolated from the cold, unforgiving Salmon, rushing by in its race to the Pacific.

If you happen to hit the springs at the right time of year, you just might spot steelhead trout (April through June) or chinook salmon (August and September) in the river, both of which spawn in this canyon. These two anadromous species — fish that spawn inland in fresh water after living out most of their lives in the salt water of the ocean — as well as the sockeyes mentioned in Ride 2, Decker Flat Loop, swim more than 800 miles upstream to arrive here.

Your out-and-back ride begins at Holman Creek Campground, on the eastern edge of the Sawtooth National Recreation Area, about 24 miles east of Stanley. This ride is along a north exposure, so it would be a good choice on a hot day. It is also at a substantially lower elevation than the other rides detailed in this chapter, so the weather is likely to be more

The Salmon River rolls out of the high country, through the timber, and into the desert.

benign here on a day when it's storming in the higher country. From here, ride west on Hwy. 75 for 1.2 miles. At this point, just before crossing a bridge which spans the Salmon, turn left onto a gravel road. At 2.0 ride across Slate Creek. As the main road curves left to follow Slate Creek, you turn right and parallel the Salmon, following a lesser-quality road marked with a dead-end sign. The early stretches of this road are quite brushed in. Until a few years ago, you could have ridden this road through all the way to O'Brien Campground and back to Hwy. 75, a total of about 11 miles. However, the Robinson Bar Resort was purchased for a private residence, the owner closed the property to public access, and this road routes directly across it.

At 3.2 miles pass by an open Douglas fir park, which offers good camping spots. At 3.4 you could spit into the Salmon — you're so close you practically are riding *in* the river. At 3.8 miles you encounter an extremely bumpy, rocky area, and at 4.1 you're looking directly across the river at Torrey's floatboat access point.

The road continues winding along on the level, with a few minor ups and downs, to 6.7, where you crest a knob and continue straight where a driveway heads right into an area of private residences. Not much farther you'll encounter a stiff uphill stretch. You can continue to about 8.0 before you hit the dead end and have to turn around and backtrack to Holman Campground. You're not likely to see any traffic on Robinson Bar Road, as it's called on the USFS maps. Perhaps because the road has been closed to through-traffic, it actually provides better mountain biking than it would otherwise. The road has been allowed to deteriorate to the point where it has become delightfully primitive!

You can learn a lesson about sniffing out good mountain-biking routes from the Robinson Bar Rd. Oftentimes, as is the case here, there are old roads on the opposite side of a river's canyon from the main highway. This holds true throughout much of the West. These roads are often like Robinson Bar Rd. featured here and Yankee Jim Rd. featured in the Yellowstone chapter — neglected, deteriorating, and relatively flat and fun to ride.

6
McCall

The area surrounding the village of McCall, Idaho, 100 miles north of Boise, is a year-round playground. Among the area's annual events are the Bear Basin Run and Mountain Bike Race, the popular McCall Winter Carnival, the New Meadows Barbecue and Loggers Show, and the National Porcupine Races.

The porcupine races, staged down the road at Council on the Fourth of July, have been a yearly happening since 1970. Two divisions (of humans) — those under 18 and those over 18 — run their "porks" for the distinction of owning the fastest porcupine in America.

McCall is also one of a handful of national centers for USFS smokejumpers. These men and women parachute into the backcountry of the western United States, providing a means of quick assistance in fire management. At their headquarters, you can take tours of the parachute

Remains of the Durden Mine, Burgdorf Hot Springs Loop

loft, the "ready room," and the aircraft used to drop the firefighters where they are needed.

In winter, downhill and cross-country skiing bring visitors to town. During the summertime, sailing and other water sports on big Payette Lake are popular, as are backpacking, stream fishing, and floating the nearby whitewater rivers. (Not far north of McCall, the Salmon River exits from the River of No Return and the Gospel Hump wilderness areas, making its final approach to the confluence with the Snake.) And mountain-biking is becoming a popular activity, as well.

Outdoor shops in town rent and sell mountain bikes. A few of the more popular riding areas near McCall include the loop around Payette Lake (which is mostly paved, but does include a few miles of gravel), Bear Basin, Sater Meadows, and Hard Creek Meadow. There are also some excellent riding opportunities in the hills to the west and south of the little town of New Meadows, which is 12 miles northwest of McCall.

One note about the mountain-biking rides to follow: If there's one word which can describe the forest roads and paths around McCall, it's *rocky*. Some roads are smoother than others of course, but generally speaking, this is the rockiest and bumpiest area featured in this guide. So, grease your knees, toughen up your rear end, and get ready to enjoy yourself. And keep an eye out for roadside porcupines — it's said they're unusually fast in these parts, and they just love to chase mountain bikers!

The supplemental maps you'll want to have on hand are available from Payette National Forest Supervisor's Office, P.O. Box 1026, McCall, ID 83638, (208) 634-8151.

1 Burgdorf Hot Springs Loop

Riding surface:	smooth and washboard gravel to extremely rocky
Beginning elevation:	6100 feet
Highest elevation:	8040 feet
Lowest elevation:	5850 feet
Distance:	26.4 miles
Relative difficulty:	hard
Time to allow:	4 to 7 hours
Best time of year:	June through September
Best time of week:	any day
Supplemental maps:	Payette National Forest Visitors Map, Payette National Forest Travel Plan Map

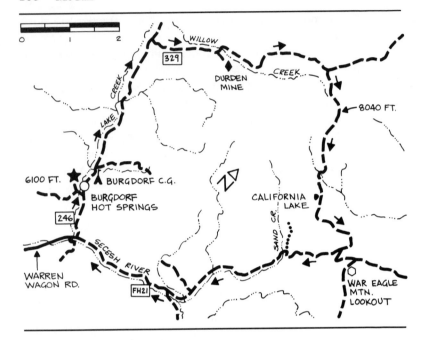

Begin your riding at Burgdorf Campground, which is immediately north of Burgdorf Hot Springs. To get to the campground, drive 28 miles northeast from McCall on Warren Wagon Road, which is paved to here, where it becomes gravel. Turn left and go 2 miles north on Forest Road 246. Save the soothing hot springs for after your ride; your body may need them!

From the campground, turn right (north) onto FR 246. If it's been dry, this wide gravel road will be like a dusty washboard. You're in the Salmon River Mountains, paralleling Lake Creek upstream. At 3.6 miles turn right onto Willow Creek Road 329 and begin a stiff uphill. This road is narrower and much more primitive than the road you just left.

Temporarily top out at 4.1. At 5.0 miles you leave the clearcut area and enter a narrow, rocky canyon. At 5.8 miles turn left at a fork in the road (by bearing right you'll come upon the remains of the old Durden Mine in 0.3 mile). The culvert which formerly carried Willow Creek beneath the road at this point has been pulled out, so you'll have to ford the stream. From here to mile 9.6, the road is closed to vehicles with more than two wheels for the purpose of soil and wildlife protection.

For the next mile-plus, you ride smoothly along the left side of Willow Creek through an aromatic meadow surrounded by large timber.

At 7.0 miles switchback to the left and begin a long, steep uphill section, which contains 30 to 40 relatively new, deep drainage ditches. Over time weather and motorcycles should pack these down, and make riding over them easier.

At 7.9 miles temporarily top out; then at 8.6 arrive at the top of the ridge. It's exhilarating ridge-riding for the next mile; at 9.6 you go around a road closure (which blocks this road from the opposite direction) and turn right at the T. At 10.3 miles bear left and continue climbing. In about a mile and a half, top out at approximately 8000 feet. From this high alpine saddle you gain spectacular views back down into the Willow Creek drainage.

At 11.9 miles start down from the saddle on a rocky, technically demanding road. At 14.1 you arrive at sparkling California Lake. A sign here warns campers to be cautious with fire because an inflammable peat bog borders the lake. Continue winding your way through the rocks on this primitive jeep road, and begin a short stretch of uphill at 15.2 miles.

At 16.0 arrive at a junction and bear right to begin a long downhill (a left turn would lead you to War Eagle Mountain Lookout). The downhill is rugged and rocky, so you can't altogether let loose on it. At 17.9 pass the trail to Kelly Meadows on your right, and at 18.0 cross a bridge spanning Sand Creek. At 18.7 you ride across another bridge, and in 0.2 mile yet another.

Burgdorf Hot Springs, a rustic resort listed on the National Register of Historic Places

At 21.8 miles bottom out and turn right onto wide (and probably a washboard) FR FH21. Follow the Secesh River upstream to 24.5, where you hit pavement, and then turn right, back onto gravel, toward Burgdorf Hot Springs. At 26.4 you return to the campground. Stop in and grab your swimsuit, and then head over to the nearby hot springs to soak your rock-rattled bones. This commercially operated, rustic resort is on the National Register of Historic Places. You'll find it a pleasant and unusual place to soak.

2 Ponderosa State Park

Riding surface:	pavement to smooth or slightly bumpy dirt
Beginning elevation:	5030 feet
Highest elevation:	5510 feet
Distance:	6.6 miles
Relative difficulty:	easy
Time to allow:	1 hour
Best time of year:	April through October
Best time of week:	during the summer, avoid weekends; any day during spring and fall
Supplemental maps:	Payette National Forest Visitors Map, Payette National Forest Travel Plan Map

Ponderosa State Park is a popular and pleasant area for outings. The parklands, 2 miles northeast of McCall, occupy a peninsula of land which juts into Payette Lake on its southeast side, nearly dividing the lake into two smaller bodies of water. Attractions here include camping, a visitor center, picnic areas, boat launches, and hiking trails which wind through stands of ancient ponderosa pine.

This is an easy ride, with a couple moderately difficult hills thrown in just to keep your shifting thumbs supple. It would make an ideal picnic ride or an outing to watch the sunset from Payette Lake Overlook. The roads you ride on are groomed as cross-country ski trails during McCall's snowy winters.

Begin at the visitor center, just inside the main entrance. Ride gradually uphill into the heart of the park on a smooth blacktop road, bearing straight ahead at 0.1 toward the day-use area (a left turn would take you into the campground).

At 0.8 mile bear left toward the scenic drive route on pavement and start a gradual downhill. At 1.1 turn right toward the picnic area and scenic drive route, and ride onto gravel in 0.1 mile. Here you have nice

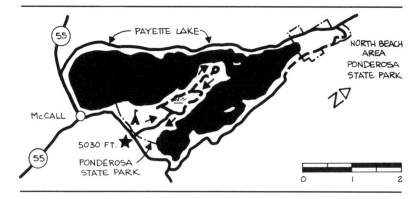

views of Payette Lake on your left. At 1.4 miles you pass by Lily Marsh on your right. Bear left on a road signed "Scenic Drive" at 1.8 (note that a right turn would lead you to Huckleberry Bay — you'll be turning here on your way down, and the junction is not signed in that direction). At 2.0 begin some roller-coaster hills, and at 2.3 miles you begin climbing in earnest. At 2.7 bear right to avoid riding the wrong way onto a one-way loop. At 3.1 you top out at Payette Lake Overlook. This is a pleasant relaxation spot, with long-range views and large trees providing shade.

At 3.2 miles begin riding downhill, and at 3.3 you start down on the road you came up. At 4.2 return to the previously mentioned junction and turn left onto Huckleberry Bay Drive. You start climbing on this narrow, rocky, heavily tree-canopied road. At 4.7 miles you encounter a steeper, very rocky uphill, and at 5.3 you top out and begin another steep downhill.

Reach the bottom of the hill at 5.5 miles, and at 5.7 you reclaim the pavement, bearing left. At 6.6 miles return to the visitor center. Because this ride's short, it could conveniently be combined with a ride to and from McCall (a round-trip of approximately 4 miles) or even with a pedal around Payette Lake (a loop of 18 miles which includes several miles of gravel along the northeast shore).

3 Brundage Mountain Loop

Riding surface:	smooth gravel to rocky and bumpy
Beginning elevation:	5090 feet
Highest elevation:	7210 feet
Distance:	19.8 or 29.5 miles
Relative difficulty:	moderate

Time to allow: 2 to 5 hours
Best time of year: June through October
Best time of week: weekdays
Supplemental maps: Payette National Forest Visitors Map, Pay-
                      ette National Forest Travel Plan Map

On Brundage Mountain's western slope is a world-class downhill ski area. This ride skirts the ski area, crosses the northern end of the mountain, climbs up its eastern side, and then circles around the southern toe of the mountain, passing through Bear Basin, probably the most popular mountain-biking area close to McCall.

From McCall, go 5 miles west on State Highway 55, and turn right onto Forest Road 257 toward Brundage Mountain Ski Area. Park and begin the ride 1 mile up this road, where FR 452 goes right. Continue riding uphill on paved FR 257.

At 2.1 miles switchback left, and at 2.6 switchback right. At 2.9, where the pavement bears right into the ski area, bear left onto gravel. This road is wide, rather bumpy, and potentially dusty. It is best to cover this long uphill stretch early in the morning when there is less chance of auto traffic and the sun isn't yet bearing down on it.

At 4.3 miles you have big views off to the left as you wrap around a cliffside. At 4.9 (that's 4.9 miles of *up*) you top out and begin a short downhill. At 5.8 go right onto FR 281 toward Brundage Reservoir and Granite Lake and begin a level to gradual downhill section. This road, although still of high grade, is somewhat rocky and narrower.

At 6.5 miles pass by Brundage Reservoir which may or may not be a dry lake bed when you do this ride. At 7.9 turn right onto FR 451 toward Hartley Meadows and Brundage Lookout (for the narrative for the 9.7-mile round-trip spur to Granite Lake, go to the end of this ride's narrative). Immediately you again begin climbing.

At 8.6 miles you cross a creek, and at 9.2 you ride into Hartley Meadows. This beautiful area studded with wildflowers offers long-range vistas. The climbing is very steep on a surface that alternates between smooth and quite loose and bumpy.

At 12.0 miles you *finally* reach the top of the long hill and pass by the turnoff to Brundage Mountain Lookout on your right (a 4-mile side-trip). You pass through some recently logged areas on this side of the divide. At 12.7 ride carefully over the diagonally positioned water bar set into the road. You head downhill through aspen, pine, and Douglas fir stands. Here, the road has a smooth, powdery surface, which would probably turn mucky when wet.

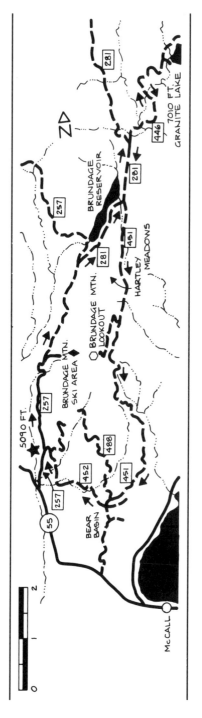

Sheep kicking up dust, Brundage Mountain Loop

At 15.5 temporarily bottom out beside a pleasant, informal camping spot on your left. Then continue down to 16.9 miles. FR 488 goes right here; you continue straight on FR 451. You're now in Bear Basin, where there are many intriguing roads and paths departing from the main road. It would be a fun area to explore on mountain bike for a full day (at least).

At 17.1 miles turn right onto FR 452. This road is smooth, narrow, and downhill; it's a cruise back to your point of origin, at 19.8.

If you choose to add on the spur to Granite Lake, back at mile 7.9 continue straight on FR 281. At 1.4 miles, where Fisher Creek Road goes left, bear right onto FR 446 toward Sater Meadows and Granite Lake. At 1.7, after crossing Fisher Creek, bear right toward Granite Lake. At 3.0 cross the East Fork of Fisher Creek. You're getting into an area where there are many spruce trees and glacially strewn granite rocks and boulders.

At 3.3 miles the road becomes bumpier and you begin to climb stiffly. At 3.6 switchback right, the first in a series of switchbacks. At 4.6 top out where FR 416 goes right; continue straight. In another 0.2 mile, turn right onto an unsigned road which brings you to Granite Lake (elevation 6734 feet) at 4.8 miles. Turn around and pedal back to the turn to Hartley Meadows, which is at 9.7 miles. Adding on the ride to Granite Lake will bring the total distance for this ride to 29.5 miles.

4 Hazard Lake–Hard Creek Loop

Riding surface:	smooth gravel to extremely rocky, unridable trail
Beginning elevation:	7050 feet
Highest elevation:	7550 feet
Distance:	7.5 miles
Relative difficulty:	hard
Time to allow:	2 to 3 hours
Best time of year:	July 16 through September; trails closed to vehicles May 1 to July 15 for erosion control
Best time of week:	any day
Supplemental maps:	Payette National Forest Visitors Map, Payette National Forest Travel Plan Map

This loop is the ride for those who simply *must* do some trail riding while in the McCall area. Those on the lookout for a technical challenge will find it here; it would take an extraordinarily talented rider to "clean" this route (that is, pedal the whole way). The ride takes you past gorgeous alpine lakes and cirques, but it isn't what you'd term a fun ride. There is a *lot* of dismounting and walking involved, primarily because this is such rocky country. Most of the grades aren't overly steep, but the rocks just keep coming at you.

Begin the ride at Hazard Lake Campground, which is 22 miles north of State Highway 55 on Brundage Mountain Road (Forest Road

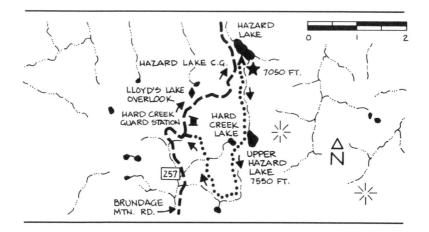

Trail riding, Hazard Lake-Hard Creek Loop

257) from a point 5 miles west of McCall. This is a picturesque USFS campground, perched on the shore of a pretty high-country lake. Ride onto the Upper Hazard Lake Trail by skirting Campsite 5. The sign here reads "Upper Hazard Lake 2; Hard Creek Lake 2½; Hard Creek Guard Stn. 5."

   The first 0.5 mile of trail is level and winds alternately through timber and meadow. It's somewhat rocky and rooty, but just a harbinger of what's to come. From 0.5 to 0.8 mile you have a technically demanding climb through the woods. From 0.8 to 1.2 miles the trail levels off again and becomes a smooth single-track through a meadow. (You may see Basque herders camped here with their sheep and work dogs. If so, as you part the flock by riding through, the strong, pungent odor of dung-dust kicked up by the sheep will temporarily obliterate the pleasant scent of pine, spruce, and wildflowers.)

   Climb from 1.3 to 1.5, and then push your bike up through the rocks from 1.5 to 1.7 miles. You'll alternately ride and walk from 1.7 to 1.9, where you arrive at Upper Hazard Lake. Bear right part way around this lake, and follow the trail signed "Hard Creek Lake 1 ½; Guard Stn. 3." It's a steep climb from 1.9 to 2.1 miles, made up primarily of pushing, with occasional ridable stretches.

Crest a rocky knob at 2.1. The rocks, roots, and ruts continuously demand that you dismount and re-mount your bike. At 2.4 miles you arrive at Hard Creek Lake, as pretty a little mountain lake as you'll find. Walk around its left bank and arrive at a sign which points you in the proper direction.

From 2.4 to 2.6 climb steeply up, then back down, following the outlet stream; at 2.7 cross the stream. From 2.7 to 3.2 miles it's downhill, but the need to get on and off your bike to get around rocks continues. For the next mile, to 4.2, it's mostly ridable through forest and sloping, sweetly scented meadow.

At 4.2 miles ride directly onto a road from the trail, and at 4.3 turn right onto FR 257. At 4.5 miles, with Hard Creek Guard Station off to your right, begin a steep uphill. At 5.1 you reach the 7190 feet summit, but a gradual uphill continues for another 0.5 mile. At 5.6 you're at Lloyd's Lake Overlook; peer down over the edge of the road, but dig your toenails in! You begin riding back downhill here. At 6.0 the downhill grade becomes steeper and continues to the campground, which you regain at 7.5 miles.

Walk your bike around domestic livestock to disturb them as little as possible.

7

The Idaho Panhandle

Many people have the impression that northern Idaho's Panhandle contains some of the wildest country remaining in the contiguous 48 states. Actually, a careful search of the Kaniksu National Forest Travel Plan Map reveals that, in the portion of the forest lying within Idaho, there are no federally designated wilderness areas. What emerges from this search is the realization that this is a forest heavily crisscrossed with logging roads and jeep trails.

The heavy timber cover which contributes to making the Panhandle so spectacular was one of the region's first attractions, and historically logging has been the primary industry. During the past century, wildlands have been continually invaded by roads, reducing the opportunities to set aside any large, unscathed blocks of land, out of reach of the chainsaw and the bulldozer. The Selkirk Crest-Long Canyon area looks like the best remaining bet for a fair-sized piece of relatively pristine wilderness.

The abundance of roads in the northern Panhandle can send the mountain biker into a babbling frenzy as he tries to determine where to go with so many options at hand. The typical ride sends the cyclist up a long drainage, across a ridge into an adjacent drainage, and then downstream on a long descent.

One exciting prospect for riders in the northern Panhandle is the possibility of spotting a woodland caribou. This animal has disappeared from the contiguous United States, except for a tiny population that survives in the southern Selkirks of northern Idaho and northeast Washington (and which ranges into southern British Columbia). Of the animals protected under The Endangered Species Act, the woodland caribou is among the most in danger. It was believed that there were only about 30 individuals in the area until the herd was augmented in 1987.

Two Panhandle towns —Bonner's Ferry and Sandpoint — serve as bases for the three rides in this chapter. Though the towns are located only 35 miles apart, they're as different from one another as night from day. Bonner's Ferry is a tiny, backwoods logging community; Sandpoint is a booming resort town, with a couple of good bicycle shops in town, at least one of which rents mountain bikes.

There are many other good mountain-biking routes in the region, in addition to those featured in this guide. For example, just south of Farragut State Park, Forest Road 209 heads east up onto the divide separating the Clark Fork and Coeur d'Alene river drainages. Forest Road 332 then meanders along this ridgeline for miles and miles, making several loop rides feasible by utilizing spur roads. You can drop off the ridge near Johnson Saddle onto Forest Road 1066 and loop back around the lakeshore, or come out on Highway 200 at the town of Clark Fork.

In the same area, an additional loop can be made by dropping down onto Coeur d'Alene River Road 306 and riding back up to the ridge on Forest Road 1533 along Buckskin Creek, to Buckskin Saddle. At Buckskin Saddle, FR 332 becomes a lower-quality road, but continues southeast along the ridgeline — once again, for miles and miles!

Another good place to mountain bike is the area surrounding Priest Lake, about 40 road miles northwest of Sandpoint. Priest Lake State Forest on the east side of the lake, and the national forest lands to the west both offer good riding.

Finally, many of the west-east running drainages coming out of the Selkirks between Sandpoint and the Canadian border offer potentially great loop rides: Highland-Roman Nose, Ruby-Caribou, and Smith-Boundary creeks, to name a few. Ride 1 is a sampler of this country.

The supplemental maps for the rides featured in this chapter are available from Supervisor's Office, Idaho Panhandle National Forests, 1201 Ironwood Drive, Coeur d'Alene, ID 83814, (208) 667-2561.

1 Myrtle–Snow Loop

Riding surface:	from pavement to smooth gravel to quite rocky and bumpy
Beginning elevation:	1800 feet
Highest elevation:	5197 feet
Distance:	33.5 miles
Relative difficulty:	hard
Time to allow:	4 to 8 hours
Best time of year:	June through September
Best time of week:	any day
Supplemental maps:	Kaniksu National Forest Visitors Map, Kaniksu National Forest Travel Plan Map

Because of the long, exposed uphill on this ride, choose a cool day or start early in the morning. Begin at the junction of Deep Creek Road and Forest Road 402/Snow Creek Road. To reach this junction from Bonner's Ferry, travel 3 miles southwest on US Highway 2/95, turn right and go 2.5 miles on County Highway 2, then turn right onto Kootenai National Wildlife Refuge (NWR) Road and go 2 miles. From Sandpoint, go 22 miles north on US 2/95 and turn left onto Deep Creek Rd./County Hwy. 2. In 6 miles, turn left onto Kootenai NWR Road. The ride begins 2 miles later, where the paved road becomes gravel. There is a Lions Club picnic ground near this junction, which is a good place to park.

Ride north on the gravel road, and enter Kootenai National Wildlife Refuge at 1.3 miles. These wet bottomlands are a far cry from the steep, timbered, high country you'll soon be encountering.

The primary purpose of the refuge is to provide habitat and resting grounds for migrating waterfowl. During the fall migration, roughly 35,000 ducks and 5000 geese pass through here. The mallard, pintail, green-winged teal, and Canada goose are among the most common species. Altogether, 224 species of birds and 45 species of mammals — including moose, elk, and black bear — have been seen on the refuge.

At 2.7 miles you bear left onto pavement and pass by the Kootenai NWR Visitor Center at 3.0. At 4.3 turn left onto an unsigned road (*after* turning onto the road you'll see a sign reading, "Snow Cr./Myrtle Cr. Loop Rd"). Start a long, steep uphill at this point. As you climb, you'll be rewarded with views of the wildlife refuge and the Cabinet and Purcell mountains across the valley.

At 6.3 miles continue straight on FR 633/Myrtle Creek Road, and

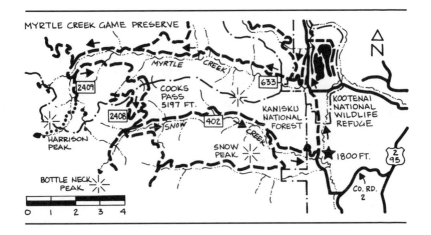

Harrison Peak dominates the view as you climb on the Myrtle-Snow Loop.

at 6.7 you enter the Kaniksu National Forest. The nearby slopes are heavily timbered with ponderosa and lodgepole pine and Douglas fir. At 7.9 the grade lessens, but soon returns to a steeper pitch, and then once again levels off at 9.7. Bear right at 11.5 miles. Now you begin to see more larch, birch, spruce, and western red cedar.

At 16.2 miles cross a creek with a pretty falls just to the right. Here in the high country, the road surface is somewhat rockier. Harrison Peak dominates the view in front of you. As the climbing continues, at 17.0 you cross Slide Creek, with a falls off to the right; at 17.3 miles you cross Myrtle Creek not far from its headwaters on the rocky flanks of Harrison Peak. There are some big hemlocks in this area.

FR 2409 goes right at 17.9 miles (this offers a good side ride and hike up to Harrison Lake). If you pedal just a little ways up FR 2409 you'll earn an expansive view of additional peaks. Back on the main route, the surface is a little rockier and more primitive than it was prior to crossing Myrtle Creek. Continuing up, you cross a bridge over Toot Creek at 19.1. At 19.5 miles the road surface becomes sandy and smooth. At 21.8 you arrive at Cooks Pass and leave the Myrtle Creek Game Preserve. After 17 miles (!) of predominantly uphill riding, you're rewarded with 12 miles of downhill. Here you have good views of Roman Nose (with a lookout on top) and Bottle Neck peaks straight ahead.

At 22.7 you pass by some recently logged slopes, and at 23.2 miles you pass FR 2408, which heads up toward Cooks Lake. At 24.4 miles turn acute left and begin following Snow Creek on a downstream scream! You pass by several roads which are not depicted on the Visitors Map, but are on the Travel Plan Map. Beginning at about 31.5, the last couple miles of downhill are very steep, with wide, sweeping turns.

Notice the cottonwoods and water birches as you return to the lowlands. At 33.5 miles you're back at the beginning point.

2 Farragut State Park

Riding surface:	pavement to dirt trail
Highest elevation:	2450 feet
Lowest elevation:	2063 feet (at the lake)
Distance:	variable
Relative difficulty:	easy
Time to allow:	1 to 4 hours
Best time of year:	April through November
Best time of week:	weekdays during the summer; any day during the spring and fall
Supplemental maps:	Kaniksu National Forest Visitors Map, Kaniksu National Forest Travel Plan Map

This 4000-acre park along the shores of Lake Pend Oreille is situated about halfway between Coeur d'Alene and Sandpoint, which are 45 miles apart. It was, in the 1940s, the site of one of the largest naval training bases in the world.

In 1950 the Idaho State Legislature in Boise approved the Idaho Fish and Game Department's application to secure the property for wildlife research and public recreation. Farragut State Park was established in 1965.

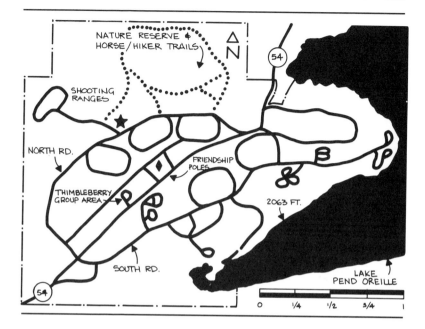

During the sailor-training period, six camps, each designed to house and train 5000 sailors at a time, were developed. Today it's hard to imagine these thousands of sailors, for the camps are now deserted. You can see their oval outlines depicted on the accompanying map. Although the buildings are long-gone, the vast road system remains. Much of what was pavement at one time has deteriorated into dirt and gravel — great for mountain biking! Many of these roads are designated bicycle paths, but they're too rugged to be properly enjoyed on skinny-tired bikes.

A lot of people camp, swim, and boat here during the summer, but most of the activity is contained along the lakefront. Spend a morning or an afternoon exploring the largely deserted old housing areas. The best places for riding are the old camps and the North and South roads, which provide access to the camps. Also pleasant are the many roads which lie between the main park road and the North Road — these pass by the amphitheatre, the Boy Scout Friendship Poles (the 1967 World Boy Scout Jamboree was held here, as were two subsequent national jamborees), and the Thimbleberry Group Area.

The following ride is a short trail outing; it represents only a fraction of the miles and time you could spend exploring Farragut State Park. This ride traverses the area shown on the accompanying map as "Nature Reserve and Horse/Hiker Trails." This is where park personnel will send

The Boy Scout Friendship Poles, Farragut State Park

you if you inquire about mountain biking, because of the low use in the area. But don't forget about the old camps — the terrain is gentle, and the riding is great.

Begin at the junction of the North Rd. and the Firing Range Road. You'll just be wandering through the woods — there is no important destination — but these trails provide fun riding. Proceed east on the North Rd., turn left at 1.0 mile, and pass through a gate. At 1.1 miles, bear right, following the directional arrow. You are riding in a forest of young lodgepole pine. The surface is mostly smooth duff, with a few rocks here and there. As you proceed you'll notice more hemlock, alder, and ferns. It's a shady and damp forest.

At 2.9 miles turn left, following the directional arrow (you can also turn right and follow this side trail out 0.7 mile to where it dead-ends). At 3.4, at the bottom of a hill in a little meadow, turn left, away from the directional arrow (the hilly trail heading to the right dead-ends at the

North Rd. in about 0.4 mile). At 3.7 you come into an area which contains some old buildings and roll onto a road on which you bear right. At 3.9 miles you return to the fork where you were at 1.1; bear right. At 4.0 turn right back onto the North Rd., and return to the beginning point at 5.0.

There are several other trails going this way and that in these woods, all of which offer fun exploring. Go out here and get lost for a while, and enjoy the trails.

3 Trestle-Lightning Loop

Riding surface: pavement to smooth gravel to rocky
Beginning elevation: 2080 feet
Highest elevation: 5000 feet
Distance: 33.8 or 46.8 miles
Relative difficulty: moderate
Time to allow: 5 to 8 hours
Best time of year: June through September
Best time of week: any day
Supplemental maps: Kaniksu National Forest Visitors Map, Kaniksu National Forest Travel Plan Map

Because of this ride's mileage, it might be prudent to arrange for a ride over the paved section, or station a car at the town of Clark Fork, and begin riding at Trestle Creek. If you do this, the mileage is 33.8. However, the 13 miles from Clark Fork to Trestle Creek are paved and the terrain is level, so it's not difficult riding. Considering the shaded nature of Trestle Creek Road, this is a good ride for a hot day.

Begin your riding by heading east up Trestle Creek Rd. 275, which begins about 14 miles southeast of Sandpoint on State Highway 200, across the road from Kamloops Resort. You start riding a gentle uphill on a relatively smooth gravel surface. At intervals there are big dips built into the road for drainage purposes — real "stomach risers."

At 5.0 miles FR 1082 goes right. Bear left, and the climbing becomes steeper. At 10.0 miles Trail 55X takes off on the left; you continue on the road. At 11.5 miles bear right, continuing on FR 275. FR 1091 goes to the left here, to Lunch Peak Lookout (a side-trip of about 5 miles). At 12.0 miles there is a junction signed "3 mi. Lightning Cr. Rd./Trestle Cr. Rd." Go left here, and begin paralleling Quartz Creek downstream. (Note: The alignment of the roads and trails in this vicinity is not shown accurately on USFS maps dated 1987 and earlier.

The map accompanying this narrative attempts to depict the actual situation.)

Bee Top–Round Top Trail 120 meets the road at this point. The sign here indicates that it is 3 miles to Trestle Peak and 8.5 to Strong Creek Road, the latter a point you can also gain access to by riding up Auxor Basin Road 489 (see mile 20.5). Sandpoint mountain-bikers note this is an excellent trail for riding — all the way to where it comes off the ridge north of the town of Clark Fork, but seek further information at one of the bike shops in Sandpoint before attempting it. As depicted on the accompanying map, this trail would make feasible two loops, one of 26 miles and a longer one of about 35 miles. (Note: Trail 120 is a National Recreation Trail open to motorcycles.)

At 15.5 miles turn right onto Lightning Creek Road 419 and follow the creek downstream. (The road going to the left at this point is signed "Moose Creek Rd./End of road 1.5 miles.") At 16.2 you pass by the trailhead to Char Creek Falls, which is 0.5 mile to your left. At 18.7 Rattle Creek Road 473 goes left, climbs over the divide, and follows Keeler and Lake creeks into Troy, Montana. Continue straight on Lightning Creek Rd.

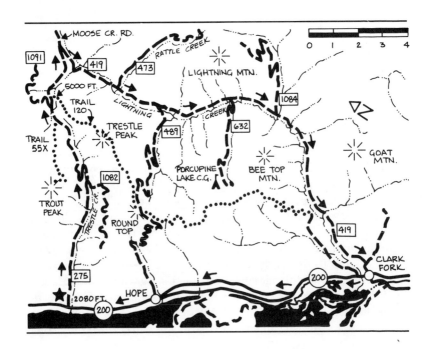

At the top of Auxor Road on the Bee Top-Round Top Divide; Lake Pend Oreille far below in the distance (Trestle-Lightning Loop)

At 20.5 Auxor Basin Rd. 489 goes right. It's a steep 9-mile climb up to the divide and Bee Top–Round Top Trail 120. This is the road you would use if you wanted to attempt one of the previously mentioned loops on Trail 120. Even if you're not going to ride the trail, pedal up this road to the divide if you can find the time and energy. It takes you to the top of the world, and the vistas you earn are grand.

Back on FR 419, at 23.7 miles, FR 632 goes right to Porcupine Lake and Campground. It would be about a 10-mile round-trip to the lake and back.

Continuing down Lightning Creek Road, FR 1084 goes left at 25.6 miles. At 33.3 miles turn right at the T, away from the cemetery and into the town of Clark Fork. At 33.8 turn right onto Highway 200. (Fish Hatchery Road is 0.5 mile west of this junction — it is 3.8 miles up this road to where Bee Top–Round Top Trail 120 comes down off the mountain. The USFS was, at this writing, in the process of obtaining a new easement for the trailhead, so check with the Sandpoint District for the current situation.)

If you're pedaling back to your car at Trestle Creek, turn right onto the frontage road at 37.2 miles. This road parallels the busier Hwy. 200 and rejoins it at 44.3. At 46.8 miles you're back at Kamloops Resort and Trestle Creek Rd.

8

Missoula

Along with a few other western communities such as Davis, California, and Eugene, Oregon, Missoula has earned a reputation as a bicyclist's town. And the cycling options surrounding this west-central Montana city *are* many and diverse: from scenic road rides to an endless array of forest paths perfect for mountain biking.

The first three rides featured here all begin close to town; there is no need to drive to the trailhead, although you could save a few miles of riding on pavement by doing so. The fourth featured ride, which begins 30 miles from town, is representative of the dozens of good riding areas within an hour's drive of Missoula.

For finding your way around and out of town, obtain the Missoula Bike Map, which can be ordered from the Missoula Bicycle Program at the city hall, 201 W. Spruce, phone 406/721-4700.

Missoula offers the usual accommodations found in a small city. There is also one commercial campground in town; USFS campgrounds are located several miles from the city.

There are several high-quality bicycle shops in Missoula. They all sell mountain bikes and have additional information on where to ride them.

Headquarters for Bikecentennial, the Bicycle Travel Association, are located in Missoula, at 113 Main St. Bikecentennial is the largest recreational cycling organization in the United States and, in addition to its many other services, acts as a clearinghouse for information on mountain biking.

Perhaps the country traversed by these rides isn't as wild as that covered in some of the other rides featured in this guide, but it is surprisingly primitive for being so close to a major city. Some areas popular for mountain biking which are not covered in the rides to follow include lands managed by the Nine Mile District of the Lolo National Forest, about 20 miles west of Missoula; Lolo Pass, an area 45 miles southwest of town which is laced with logging roads; and Lubrecht State Experimental Forest, 25 miles east of the city. Lubrecht contains a system of tree-canopied paths which double as ski trails in winter and mountain-biking trails during the snowless months. A privately owned cross-country skiing center, Nightingale Nordic, is up Graves Creek, near the Lumberjack Saloon (see Ride 4). Their trails are ideal for mountain biking.

While you're exploring the forests around Missoula, reflect on this community's long history of mountain biking. In 1897 U.S. Army Lieutenant James A. Moss departed from Fort Missoula with 20 men of the Twenty-fifth Infantry Corps, a group of black soldiers. They were headed all the way to St. Louis on balloon-tire bicycles (the chain-driven bicycle had been invented only 18 years earlier). Moss, a cycling enthusiast, was out to prove to General Nelson A. Miles that the bicycle could become a viable means of transportation for troops.

The roads separating Missoula and St. Louis at that time were largely mud trails and sand paths winding through the wilds. The Twenty-fifth accomplished the 1900-mile ride in 41 days, for an average of 46 miles per day — a respectable pace for a cyclist today, on pavement! The weather, bad water, and rough country combined to make the trip extremely difficult. Many of the soldiers had never even been on a bike before, making their accomplishments all the more admirable. Though the journey was successful, the Army never did designate bicycle troops; Lieutenant Moss was ordered back to Fort Missoula. Perhaps he'd take solace in the fact that Missoula today is a bicycling Mecca.

The supplemental map you'll want for the Missoula area is available from Lolo National Forest, Missoula Ranger District, Building 24-A, Fort Missoula, Missoula, MT 59801, (406) 329-3814.

1 Mount Sentinel Loop

Riding surface:	pavement to somewhat rocky trails
Beginning elevation:	3210 feet
Highest elevation:	5158 feet
Distance:	24.7 miles
Relative difficulty:	moderate
Time to allow:	3 to 6 hours
Best time of year:	April through October
Best time of week:	any day
Supplemental maps:	Lolo National Forest Visitors Map, Lolo National Forest Travel Plan Map

Mount Sentinel, as its name suggests, stands watch over Missoula. It's a long, roundabout ride to the top, but it's effort well spent. And, the coast down is marvelous!

Begin riding on the old Milwaukee Road railroad grade at Jacob's

Riding on the Pattee Canyon Ski Trails, Mount Sentinel Loop

Island Park, on the south side of the footbridge at the north edge of the University of Montana campus. Here you ride east on the wood-chip path, following the Clark Fork River upstream into the Hellgate Canyon.

The wood-chip trail soon becomes dirt, and at 0.3 mile you pass through a gate signed "No Motor Vehicles." At 0.5 mile enter the Kim Williams Nature Area, dedicated in 1987 to the memory of Missoula naturalist and National Public Radio commentator Kim Williams. This city park is a designated recreation corridor for hiking, jogging, horseback riding, and mountain biking.

Occasionally, you pass by some good waterfowl-viewing areas in river backwaters. On your right are steep slopes and rocky draws; you'll see evidence of the fire that raged in the canyon, on Mount Sentinel's north side, in the summer of 1985. The timber on your right is mostly Douglas fir, western larch, and ponderosa pine, and along the river on your left is cottonwood.

At 3.1 miles you leave the Kim Williams Nature Area. A railroad bridge spanning the river on your left brings the tracks in beside you. At 4.2 miles, at a road crossing, turn right onto gravel Deer Creek Road. At 4.3 you begin climbing a steep hill. At 4.9 cross a cattle guard and begin a rolling section of terrain. At 6.0 miles, after a downhill section, start uphill again; a large set of power lines is on your left.

At 7.3 miles the power lines veer upslope as you ride up a long, gradual hill through pleasant forest, with an occasional private home on your right. There are some very large ponderosa pine and larch in this vicinity. At 9.5 miles you switchback hard right. There are two roads coming in from your left here; just bear all the way to the right on the main road.

At 9.9 miles the road becomes level to slightly downhill. At 10.7 miles, immediately after hitting pavement, turn left into the gravel parking area. In approximately 100 yards turn left toward the gate, rather than following the road around as it loops right. At 10.8, just before the "Road Closed" sign and the gate, veer right onto a trail.

At 10.9 turn right onto the primitive road and immediately turn left uphill, following the ski-trail markers. Just around the next corner, where the ski-trail markers direct you steeply upslope, bear right instead on the other apparent trail, which shortly becomes a primitive road. (Note: These ski trails are recommended for mountain biking during the summer. The blue trail is a very fun loop of 3.5 miles. Ski trails are off-limits here — as everywhere — once the snow falls in autumn or early winter. It's also important to note that there is some extensive work slated for these trails during 1989 or 1990, which will affect their layout. Regardless, it will still be possible to follow trails to the point noted below, at mile 11.8. Or, you can just follow the pavement from 10.7 miles to that point, as well.)

At 11.8 miles pass through a gate and turn left onto the pavement, then immediately turn right through another gate onto unsigned Crazy Canyon Road (or you can continue downhill on the pavement, joining the narrative below at 18.5 miles, reducing the total distance of this ride by 6.7 miles). Crazy Canyon Rd. is generally closed to car traffic, although the USFS permits members of the local hang-glider club to drive up it for their flights off Mount Sentinel. Mountain bikes are always permitted.

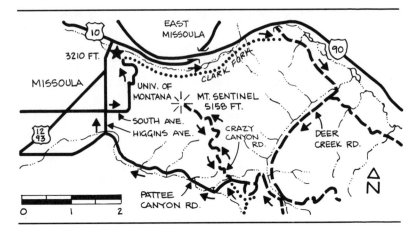

Simply keep following the beaten path. The first 1.4 miles are gradually uphill along a smooth surface; then, at 13.2, it steepens into a first-gear hill. At 13.9 miles curve sharp left around a drainage and start up a very steep, 0.1 mile-long hill.

At 14.7 bear right at the fork onto the similar-surfaced road. At 14.9 miles you enter an area where the road evidently acted as a firebreak during the 1985 Hellgate Burn. Notice burned trees upslope to your right, and unburned forest on your left. At 15.1 pass through a gate, and at 15.2 you encounter a hill so steep that it's doubtful *anyone* could ride up it. If you do try, be careful not to tip over backwards!

You'll probably end up climbing this final stretch of road to the top of Mount Sentinel on foot and either pushing your bike or stashing it in the woods at the base of the hill. It's only about 0.3 mile to the top from here, so be sure and climb to it even though you're not able to ride all the way. From here it's a grand view of all of Missoula and the mountains ringing the town.

Turn around and ride back down Crazy Canyon Rd., using caution as you cross the several large drainage ditches which cross it. At 18.5 miles again pass through the gate onto the pavement and turn right onto Pattee Canyon Road. It's a smooth, fun descent back into town. At 22.1 miles, at the stop sign, turn right onto Higgins Avenue. At the stop light at 22.7, turn right and follow South Avenue until it curves left and becomes Maurice Avenue at 23.2. At 23.7 turn right onto Beckwith (riding straight would take you onto the University of Montana campus), which curves left and becomes Campus Drive. At 24.7 miles you arrive back at your beginning point.

2 Rattlesnake Out and Back

Riding surface: smooth to very rocky and bumpy
Beginning elevation: 3600 feet
Highest elevation: 5100 feet
Distance: 30 miles
Relative difficulty: moderate
Time to allow: 5 to 8 hours
Best time of year: May through October
Best time of week: weekdays
Supplemental maps: Lolo National Forest Visitors Map, Lolo
                     National Forest Travel Plan Map

This ride is special; the best that Missoula has to offer. You're on an old road the entire way — a path which used to provide access to several homesteads along Rattlesnake Creek, as well as to logging areas deeper in the wilds. Indeed, during the first few miles you'll spot some signs of previous occupation: Here and there you'll see old apple trees, rock piles from the days of meadow clearing, and even an occasional wayward, rusty auto-body part.

However, the unique aspect of this ride begins just beyond the 8.5-mile point. Here, you begin pedaling through a corridor literally *surrounded* by wilderness. When the Rattlesnake National Recreation Area and Wilderness (RNRAW) was created in 1980, this road and its narrow corridor were excluded from the wilderness boundaries. USFS and Montana Department of Fish, Wildlife and Parks personnel occasionally drive it for various administrative purposes. The general public is not allowed to drive on this road, but mountain bikes are permitted. If possible, do this ride on a weekday, as weekend use can be heavy in the Rattlesnake.

The RNRAW contains many high lakes, a lot of which hold good fishing opportunities. A popular combination trip here is to pedal the approach to a trailhead (carrying a small pack), stash your bike in the woods near the trailhead, and walk into the wilderness for a long day-hike or an overnight. Biking in dramatically reduces the amount of time spent on the approach. A strong rider can get all the way to the end of the corridor in 2 hours. The same 15 miles would make a long day's hike. You could ride in first thing in the morning, do a ten-mile-loop hike along with some fishing, then ride back out in the afternoon, albeit somewhat tiredly!

You may want to purchase the excellent Rattlesnake National

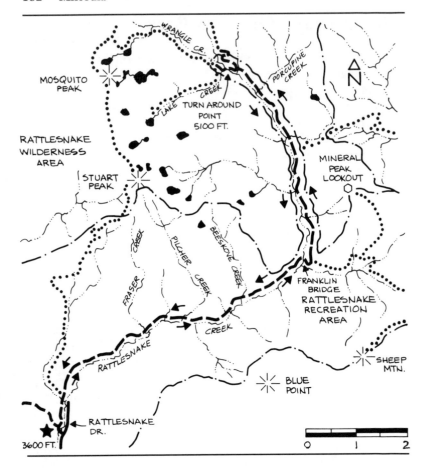

Recreation Area and Wilderness Map for this ride, especially if you plan to do some hiking while up the Rattlesnake. Produced by geography students at the University of Montana, it is widely available at stores in Missoula.

For this trip, begin at the RNRAW trailhead, which is 4 miles north of the Interstate 90–Van Buren Street interchange. Go north on Van Buren, which becomes Rattlesnake Drive, and turn left onto gravel at the sign pointing toward the recreation area.

The road you're pedaling on is generally uphill, with some steep and rolling sections. At first smooth, the road soon becomes quite rocky. It again becomes smooth in the 2.0 vicinity. You ride through a heavy forest cover of ponderosa pine and Douglas fir, with high cliffs to your right, across Rattlesnake Creek.

At 2.7 miles, ride up and over a terminal moraine, evidence of the glacier which carved out the valley and receded only about 12,000 years ago. At 3.7 miles you cross Fraser Creek. Anywhere past the three-mile-zone boundary, which you cross at this point, camping is permitted. The USFS urges campers to utilize existing primitive sites.

At 4.7 you encounter a rocky stretch and then cross Pilcher Creek at 4.9; the riding again becomes smoother. From 5.7 to 6.2 you skirt the base of a large talus slope, which creates very bumpy riding conditions. Enter a large meadow at 6.5, and cross Beeskove Creek at 6.6. Beyond this point, Rattlesnake Creek is open to fishing (catch and release, using artificial lures only). The creek was Missoula's primary water source until a severe outbreak of giardiasis in the early 1980s. So now the water and its users — especially man and other mammals, such as beavers and smaller rodents — are monitored.

Coasting through a stand of western larch, Rattlesnake Out and Back

Just beyond Beeskove Creek, the Rattlesnake Wilderness Area closes in on your left. At 8.5 miles cross roaring Rattlesnake Creek on Franklin Bridge and immediately begin a long uphill. If you want a shorter ride or don't want to tackle the more difficult riding conditions ahead, Franklin Bridge is a good turn-around point.

At this point, the wilderness joins in on your right. From here on, you can nearly throw a rock into the wilderness area, but you're never *in* the wilderness. Actually, this road is about the only place in the area that is flat enough to make riding feasible. The Rattlesnake Wilderness, like many other wilderness areas, was set aside, ultimately, because its extreme terrain made it impractical for man's commercial activities and exploitation. Even if it were not wilderness, common sense would prevent you from riding off the road and onto the surrounding, steep trails.

At 8.8 miles you pass by the trailhead to Mineral Peak/Sheep Mountain on your right. At 9.0 to 9.3, still heading uphill, you're bisecting an immense talus slope as you ride atop a platform chiseled through the field of boulders. The riding is quite bumpy. The road levels off at 9.8 miles and becomes gradually downhill to 10.3, where you again come in alongside the creek. Impressive cliffs surround you as you pass through stands of giant larch. If you have the pleasure of doing this ride after mid-October, in some areas you'll find yourself pedaling on a carpet of golden larch needles.

At 11.6 miles the West Fork Gold Creek Trail takes off to the right. At 12.5 the road becomes quite rocky once again. Cross Porcupine Creek on a wooden bridge at 13.2. At 14.6 miles bear left downhill on the main road where a lesser-quality road goes up to the right. You arrive at Wrangle Bridge, which spans Rattlesnake Creek, at 15.0. The creek is exceptionally pretty in here, rushing through steep-sided rock walls and forming several stair-stepping pools along the way. Note that the country suddenly opens up into a big basin as you approach this spot. Here three major drainages merge — Lake Creek, Wrangle Creek, and Rattlesnake Creek. Trails follow each of these creeks up to wilderness lakes.

Turn around at Wrangle Bridge. Technically, the wilderness area doesn't begin until 0.3 mile farther, but the riding becomes quite steep once past the bridge. If you do wander up this hill, on your way back down you'll see the fire lookout high atop distant Mineral Peak straight ahead. You'll notice the rocks and bumps more during your descent; ride carefully and slowly through the extremely rocky and loose sections.

For nearly its entire distance, this ride is in a steep-sided canyon, 1 to 2 miles wide, so long-range vistas are uncommon. However, the precipitous rock walls, the stands of huge virgin timber, and potential opportunities to spot elk, mountain goats, black bears, cougars, and bald eagles will have you asking yourself, "Am I really only a few miles from busy Missoula, Montana?"

3 Blue Mountain Loop

Riding surface:	smooth to somewhat bumpy gravel and loose dirt trails
Beginning elevation:	3300 feet
Highest elevation:	6460 feet
Distance:	21.3 or 26.7 miles
Relative difficulty:	short loop — hard; long loop — moderate
Time to allow:	4 to 7 hours
Best time of year:	June through October
Best time of week:	weekdays during the summer; any day during the fall
Supplemental maps:	Lolo National Forest Visitors Map, Lolo National Forest Travel Plan Map

The Missoula Ranger District of the Lolo National Forest has officially designated Blue Mountain Recreation Area as a mountain-bike use area. The multiple-use plan for Blue Mountain defines seven trail-user classes: A — four-wheel drive; B — three- and four-wheeled all-terrain vehicles; C — motorcycles; D — bicycles; E — horses; F — hikers; and G — handicapped.

Each trail is marked with one of the above letters. The activity designated by that letter, as well as all of the activities after that letter — but not before it — can be carried out on that particular trail. For instance, D trails are open to bicycles, horses, hikers, and handicapped, but not open to motorcycles or three- and four-wheeled motor vehicles.

Blue Mountain is a wonderful playground close to Missoula that holds some great mountain-biking opportunities. It has additional mountain-biking trails not mentioned in the featured ride, but indicated on the accompanying map. Several of the roads and trails continue off the edge of the map, so use it in association with the supplemental map listed at the beginning of this description.

During the week you won't run into many trailbikes or other ORVs, even on their designated trails. However, there can be a fair number of them on Blue Mountain during the summer weekends. There are some pleasant campsites up near the lookout, and the views at sunset and sunrise are splendid. Just remember to bring plenty of water if you'll be camping near the top. And, again, the USFS urges you to use an existing primitive site, rather than create a new one.

To get to the trailhead, go south on US Highway 93 to the southern edge of town. At the junction with Blue Mountain Road, turn right. In 0.5 mile, where the pavement curves right, turn into the parking area and begin the ride there. Continue on the main road as it curves and becomes gravel.

At 0.7 mile, after cresting a moderate hill and starting down, turn left onto Forest Road 365. You pass by a large signboard on your right which depicts the Blue Mountain Recreation Area. Start up on this wide gravel road.

At 1.7 miles pass through the first of two opened gates, and at 2.5 switchback left. Here you are afforded good views of the Missoula Valley on your left. At 3.5 switchback left once again. At 3.8 a signed mountain-bike trail takes off to the left; you continue up the main road, which switches back to the right in 0.1 mile. At this point two trails go to the left — one motorcycle and one ORV trail.

At 4.2 you are presented with good views of the Rattlesnake National Recreation Area and Wilderness directly to your right. At 5.2 miles you switchback left and pass through the second open gate. The grade becomes less steep at this point. At 6.0 you crest a saddle; however, you don't reap the benefits ordinarily associated with crossing a divide — here, you must continue uphill along the mountainside!

At 7.2 miles curve hard left around the head of a drainage. The terrain is quite level up to 8.3, where you curve left through another drainage and again begin up. At 8.9 miles you curve sharp right, continuing up. At 9.9 you have superb views, down through the Hayes Creek drainage, of the Missoula Valley far below, as well as of the Rattlesnake and Mission mountains. You'll begin noticing that tall, straight spruce trees are supplanting the pine and larch of the lower elevations.

At 11.0 miles curve hard right through a drainage, and at 11.5 turn acute left off the main road onto a road which switchbacks above the main one. This is the lookout approach road; it is somewhat narrower and steeper, but still of high quality. At 12.6 miles switchback right, and at 12.8 note a trail taking off to your left — this is the one you'll ride onto on your way down if you choose to ride the loop rated hard.

At about 100 yards past the trail, note the road coming in off the ridgetop on your right. This is the road you ride down from the lookout if you've chosen the harder loop. At 13.1 miles there is a road going left; continue straight. At 13.9 pass through a gate, and at 14.0 switchback to

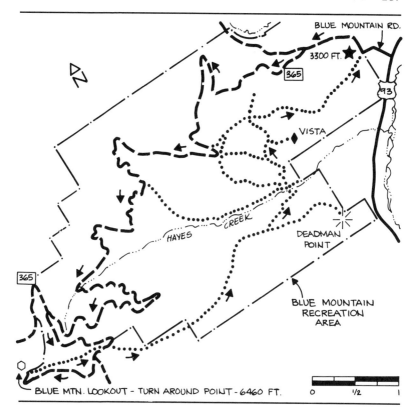

the right. At 14.2 a switchback to the left leads you immediately up to the lookout. Departing from the right side of this switchback is the road you'll turn onto if you choose the more difficult route down.

If, however, you want to keep this a non-technical ride, with a fun, cruiser of a downhill, then ride back down the main road to mile 24.6 and turn right onto the mountain-bike trail mentioned at mile 3.8 on your way up. Then follow this path back to your beginning point, bringing the total to 26.7.

If you'd prefer a technical challenge, and the opportunity to see some new country, follow this route down: Turn onto the previously mentioned road at the switchback at 14.2 miles. To give you some idea of the steepness of the terrain you're about to encounter, it is 7.1 miles back to your point of origin going this way — barely more than half the distance of riding back on the road.

At 14.3 bear left, continuing down, rather than heading up onto the point of rocks. At 14.4 bear right uphill at the fork, then left, away from the road that goes to the visible domed structure. At 14.5, after a short walking stretch, start down and bear right on the more beaten path. The trail winds in and out among rock and timber and then heads steeply down along the ridge.

At 15.1 turn left onto the main road, and in about 100 yards, turn right onto the trail previously mentioned at mile 12.8. This trail immediately crests a small knob and heads into the timber, winding down Deadman Ridge, sometimes through very loose dirt. At 15.6 miles you hit a short uphill stretch. At 15.7 switchback left across a radically steep slope, which should be walked.

After a steep, ridable stretch, at 16.9 and at 17.4 you encounter very loose, short downhill sections where you have to dismount and walk. It's smooth, clear sailing to 17.9, where you bear left downhill at the Y. At 18.6 you come into a fenced-in creek bottom (the post-and-pole fences were designed to keep ORVs out of the stream and off the banks). Cross Hayes Creek; when you exit the fenced-in area at 18.7 miles, you're faced with a four-way junction. Don't go hard right, along the fence line, which follows Hayes Creek; rather, turn right 45 degrees onto a trail signed by the USFS as easiest for motorcycles.

Commence pushing your bike for 0.1 mile up this "easiest" trail! You have a steep, but ridable, section to 18.9 and another short walker at 19.0. At 19.2 bear right onto a trail signed as a more difficult bicycle trail. At 19.4 miles, after cresting a small hill, begin down on a gently graded, double-track road.

At 19.5 miles you encounter another "more difficult" bicycle trail, which goes right to Vista Point; you continue straight onto a "most difficult" bicycle trail. (This designation is a misnomer when you're going in this direction, for it's all downhill and very easy riding.) At 19.6 a horse trail crosses your path; you continue straight on the bicycle trail.

At 19.7 arrive at a bicycle trail, onto which you turn right (the path you're turning off of becomes a horse trail, which is off-limits to bicycles). At 20.5 miles you burst out of the timber and back into the grasslands, and at 21.3 you pass through the gate back to your beginning point.

4 Howard-Graves Loop

Riding surface:	generally smooth gravel
Beginning elevation:	3788 feet
Highest elevation:	5650 feet
Distance:	27.2 miles
Relative difficulty:	moderate

Time to allow: 2 to 5 hours
Best time of year: May through October
Best time of week: any day
Supplemental maps: Lolo National Forest Visitors Map, Lolo
                      National Forest Travel Plan Map

This fun loop takes you through some drainages still relatively virgin and heavily timbered, for being so close to Missoula. To get to the beginning point, head south out of Missoula on US Highway 93. In the town of Lolo, at 9 miles, turn right up US Highway 12. The Graves Creek turnoff, which is also signed as the turnoff to the Lumberjack Saloon, is 16 miles from Lolo. Park here, and begin riding west on US 12, which is a section of the TransAmerica Bicycle Trail.

At 2.3 miles, turn right onto Howard Creek Road 238, just across from the Lolo Work Center. (Englishmen riding the TransAmerica Bicycle Trail sometimes become confused and amused here when they see the signs pointing toward Lolo W.C. To them, "W.C." stands for "water closet," or restroom!)

Begin up this drainage on a moderately graded, smooth road. At first you're surrounded by timber, but in the 6-mile range you enter Howard Creek Meadows. (At 7.0 Tepee Creek Road goes right, a potential alternative route which is quite a bit shorter and steeper.)

At 9.0, at the upper reaches of the meadows, the grade steepens. At 10.6 miles you arrive at a junction on a divide. Turn right toward Graves

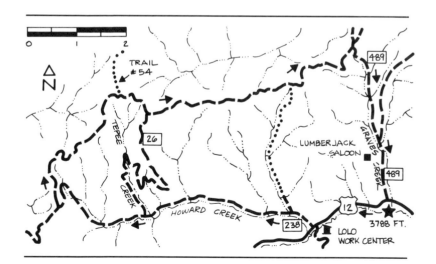

Creek, continuing uphill along the ridgetop. (A left turn would take you to Fish Creek and the Lewis and Clark Highway — which is the old name for Highway 12.) At 12.6 miles you temporarily top out and start a flat-to-downhill section. From this point to about 20 miles, you'll be crossing from side to side of a ridgetop, resulting in a roller-coaster effect. Keep an eye out for open-top water bars which have been implanted in the road for drainage purposes. Spanning the road diagonally, some are wide enough to catch a tire in.

At 15.1, after a long stretch of uphill, you arrive at the Petty Creek/ Fish Creek Divide. Trail 54 to Deer Peak goes left; you continue on the road. At 16.2, the road from Howard Creek Meadows, which goes up Tepee Creek, comes in on the right (it's signed "Tepee Ridge Trail 26").

At around 17.0, you have good views into the South Fork of Petty Creek (peek through the trees), and at 17.5 you're afforded views of an expansive, heavily timbered drainage on the right. At 18.1 cross over the ridge after a 0.7-mile climb. You soon begin a long stretch of downhill.

At 21.2 miles you pass the trailhead to the North Fork Howard Creek Trail, off to the right. Continue down through some open ponderosa pine parks to a stop sign at the junction at 23.1. Turn right onto Graves Creek Road 489 (the road you're coming off of is signed "Wagon Mountain Road" at this point). Ride down through the timber and meadows along Graves Creek, and at 25.7 miles arrive at the Lumberjack Saloon. This unique watering hole is definitely worth a visit. Continue down the road to 27.2, where you return to your point of origin.

9
The North Fork
of the Flathead River

$\mathcal{T}$he Flathead River's North Fork defines the western boundary of Glacier National Park. The river runs from Canada, across the international border, and 50 miles south, to where it joins the Flathead's Middle Fork near Hungry Horse, Montana. The North Fork drains much of the western half of the park, as well as the east slope of the Whitefish Range, which lies to the west of the river. This backwoods corner of Montana holds a wealth of mountain-biking opportunities, both in the Flathead National Forest on the west side of the river and, to the east, within Glacier National Park.

Yes, *within* the national park. The northwest corner of this "crown of the lower 48" contains some 50 miles of primitive gravel roads open to vehicles, including mountain bikes. The really wonderful thing is that very few cars or trucks venture into this remote section of the park. This area may not be entirely undiscovered, but it is largely unvisited. (The 35,000-acre Red Bench fire of 1988 changed the face of much of the country around Polebridge. It also may result in growing numbers of visitors, as the NPS plans to encourage park users to see the area and witness the regeneration of the forest.)

One of the featured rides is within Glacier National Park. The other two take place in the Flathead National Forest and the adjacent Stillwater State Forest. There are several USFS and NPS campgrounds in the area which can provide pleasant base camps. However, if the prospect of camping out among one of the heaviest concentrations of grizzly bears in the contiguous 48 states doesn't appeal to you, you can base out of the rustic youth hostel in Polebridge, a small town about 40 miles north of Kalispell.

In addition to bears, keep an eye out for elk, moose, mountain goats, cougars, and bighorn sheep. The wolf also has recently made a comeback in the North Fork.

Rocky Mountain goat, an inhabitant of Glacier National Park and other areas in the Northern Rockies

Because this is big timber country, check ahead with the USFS to see if there are any logging operations under way near where you'll be riding (not a concern if riding in Glacier National Park). There usually is some logging in progress somewhere in the North Fork, but it's a huge area. Stay off the main North Fork Road, as it's the primary artery leading to the mills.

There are good bike shops in both Whitefish and Kalispell which sell mountain bikes and gear and provide information on additional riding possibilities. A few suggestions include the 25-mile Inside Road, which goes northwest from Fish Creek Campground on Lake McDonald to the river crossing at Polebridge. This easy ride over a primitive gravel road is entirely within Glacier National Park. Some long loops through very scenic country can be accomplished by riding up the drainages near the Canadian border — Trail Creek and Thoma Creek. These cross the Whitefish Divide into the Kootenai National Forest to the west, where you're greeted with another endless array of rides from which to choose.

The supplemental map you'll need for the featured rides, as well as dozens of other potentially good routes, is available from Flathead National Forest, Glacier View Ranger Station, Box W, Columbia Falls, MT 59912, (406) 892-4372.

1 Lookout Loop

Riding surface: smooth dirt and gravel with some talus
Beginning elevation: 3741 feet
Highest elevation: 5982 feet
Distance: 21.7 miles
Relative difficulty: hard
Time to allow: 3 to 8 hours
Best time of year: July through October
Best time of week: any day
Supplemental map: Flathead National Forest Visitors Map (north half)

From Polebridge, go 10 miles north on the North Fork Road to Ford Work Center. The ride begins at the junction of the North Fork Rd. and Forest Road 318. Ride west on FR 318, heading gradually upstream.

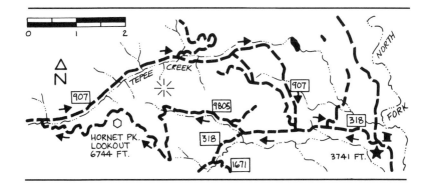

At 2.1 miles pass by FR 907 on your right. At 3.4 turn right onto FR 9805 toward Hornet Mountain/Tepee Creek. Here you begin a very steep climb of about 5 miles. You're climbing up and over the ridge which separates the Whale Creek and Tepee Creek drainages.

At 5.6 switchback to the left and then to the right at 6.7 miles. Where the climb tops out at 8.6 miles and you'll naturally stop to recover, there is a pullout and an abandoned road on the right. Rest a minute here, hide your bike in the woods, and hike up the trail which begins on the other side of the road. It's a stiff hoof of between 1 and 2 miles, but the old Hornet Peak Lookout, at 6744 feet, is worth the effort.

Originally constructed in 1922, this is the only "D-1 Standard" fire lookout still standing. USFS pioneers built the lookout mostly from native materials: They used crosscut saws to down on-site timber, they squared the logs and fit corners with broad axes, and with froes they split shingles for the roof. Today, the lookout is being restored by the North Fork Preservation Association.

From atop Hornet Peak you can see the long glacial lakes, which adorn the west side of the park, and many of Glacier's high peaks. These mountains began as sediments settling out of an ancient sea about 600 million years ago. Lime, mud, and then sand built up into thick layers. Around 60 million years ago, tensions within the earth's crust began folding and breaking the sedimentary layers. These pressures, which lasted for millions of years, finally resulted in a section of crust 300 miles long being thrust 75 miles to the east. This produced the Lewis Overthrust of Glacier and Waterton Lakes (Canada's counterpart just to the north) national parks. The rock was folded and broken and subsequently eroded by water into a mountain range. Then, relatively recently in the geological timetable, glaciers accomplished the "finish work"; and today we reap the benefits — these highly sculpted peaks are among the most beautiful in the world.

When you finally pull yourself away from the views, catch your breath and hold onto it, for the coming descent will do its best to take it away. It's one of the most fun downhills you'll find. It begins gently and eases into a steep, but never treacherous, pitch. The many curves in the road are wide-angled enough that you can keep your speed up riding through them.

After 3 miles of downhill, at 11.6 miles, you cross Tepee Creek. Turn right at the T onto FR 907 (if you want to explore, you can turn left, but the road dead-ends in about 2 miles). The downhill mellows a bit

Hornet Peak Lookout, the only "D-1 standard" lookout still standing

here, but it continues for another 7 miles, rolling toward the end through a stand of giant western larch, that tall, straight conifer which turns golden and loses its needles in the autumn.

At 16.6 miles you pass by a lesser-quality road on your right; if you feel the urge to explore a bit, you can try this option — it will rejoin FR 907 farther down the road. If not, just continue straight on FR 907. At 19.4 you'll see the road mentioned above join FR 907 on your right; at 19.6 turn left at the T back onto FR 318. At 21.7 miles you're back at Ford Work Center.

Note: If someone in your party is willing to drive the car back to Polebridge, the others can pedal back. It's a pleasant, rolling ride of approximately 18 miles to Polebridge on the forest roads which parallel the main North Fork Rd. to the west. To begin, turn *right* at mile 19.6 noted above. The roads you'll use — and you'll absolutely need the supplemental map listed to do this — are Forest Roads 318, 1671, 210C, 1675A, 115, 1685, and 376.

2 Kintla Lake Out and Back

Riding surface:	smooth dirt
Beginning elevation:	3543 feet
Highest elevation:	4008 feet
Distance:	29 miles
Relative difficulty:	easy

Time to allow: 4 to 8 hours
Best time of year: May through October
Best time of week: weekdays during summer; any day during
                      spring and fall
Supplemental map: Flathead National Forest Visitors Map (north
                      half)

This special ride takes place entirely on roads within Glacier National Park (except for the first and last mile). Whereas the Lookout Loop is a thrilling ride which gets you into the high spruce basins, the Kintla Lake Out and Back is a gentle ride, conducive to stopping often to admire the beautiful country or perhaps scan the river for a bald eagle. It passes through open meadows on the North Fork's floodplain and through thick forests of Douglas fir and hemlock. It is best done first thing in the morning or late in the afternoon, when the chances of spotting wildlife are greatest. Along this road you'll see plenty of deer, perhaps a black bear, and maybe even a rare wolf.

In 1984, University of Montana forestry professor Robert Ream heard something which he had hoped to hear for a long time — wolves howling. Since he began studying wolves in Montana in 1973, he had neither heard nor seen one in the state. The howling he heard came from what was eventually dubbed the Magic Pack, after its Houdini-like talent for disappearing every time scientists believed they knew where to find them. Since then, female members of the pack have given birth to pups in this area; in fact, you may find the Kintla Lake Road closed during parts of the spring, in order to protect the wolf families during the sensitive whelping period.

Begin your riding in the hamlet of Polebridge, and follow the road that goes toward Glacier Park. At 1.0 mile, cross the North Fork into the park. Turn left toward Kintla Lake; there's no reasonable way to get off-track from this point on.

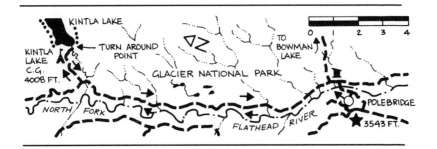

Hidden Lake, one of many treasures of Glacier National Park accessible by parking your bike and hiking

For the next several miles, you ride through alternating open meadow and timber. The riding is quite flat as you ride through Big Prairie and Round Prairie. At several points along your way — in the vicinities of 6, 8, 9, 10, 11, and 12 miles — you encounter bends in the river and are afforded open views of the Wild and Scenic waterway and the Whitefish Range to the west. After the final river-bend, at 12.0, veer northeast away from the North Fork, cross Kintla Creek, and begin paralleling the creek upstream through thick woods.

At 14.5 miles you arrive at the Kintla Lake Campground. The classic glacial lake stretches 5 miles up to the base of the high peaks, but is less than a mile at its widest. If it's particularly warm out, a swim might feel good. It will certainly cool you off, if nothing else! It would be fun to have a fire here and cook breakfast, or supper if you're doing this as a late afternoon ride. It's a great place to sit and listen for the howling wolves and to scare yourself by telling bear stories.

Paralleling the North Fork of the Flathead River, Kintla Lake Out and Back

Turn around and retrace your tread tracks back to Polebridge. If you have the time and energy, just before crossing the bridge back into town, take a left and ride the 5 miles to Bowman Lake, which is every bit as pretty as Kintla. This will add a total of 10 miles and another 400 feet of climbing to the ride. If you're looking for other diversions, there are some good trails for hiking (*not* riding) along the banks of both lakes.

3 North Fork–Whitefish Point to Point

Riding surface:	smooth to very rocky and bumpy
Beginning elevation:	3970 feet
Highest elevation:	5611 feet
Lowest elevation:	3027 feet
Distance:	40.9 miles
Relative difficulty:	moderate
Time to allow:	5 to 8 hours
Best time of year:	June through October
Best time of week:	any day
Supplemental map:	Flathead National Forest Visitors Map (north half)

It may be hard to decide who in your party will drive to Whitefish to pick you up at the end of this ride, for it's a gem. If you want to leave your car at Polebridge, you could do this ride on one day, and then return the next by winding around on the roads which take you behind the Big Mountain Ski Area and lead you to Big Creek Campground, just south of Polebridge. From Big Creek you could then ride to Polebridge on the roads which are to the west of Demers and Winona ridges (this route will become clear if you study your Visitors Map).

Or, if you find yourself in Whitefish without an automobile, doing this North Fork–Whitefish ride in reverse would be a good way to get to the heart of the excellent riding country without the need for a car.

From Polebridge drive 4 miles north on the North Fork Road (or pedal it in relative calm by leaving Polebridge before 7:00 A.M.). Begin riding west on Forest Road 115/Red Meadow Road, which is a high-quality, smooth gravel road. You'll climb steadily but gradually up to placid Red Meadow Lake, which is at 11.2 miles. Stop now and then to scan the many open slopes — they're a good place to spot a grizzly. And this is how you want to see them, from a distance!

At 1.3 miles you pass by a road which takes off on your right, then one at 1.7 (Moose Creek Road), and another which goes left at 1.9 (FR 1685). There are several other primitive paths which take off from the main road during the next 9 miles, all of them beckoning you to turn off and explore.

Reading up on the local geology, North Fork-Whitefish Point to Point

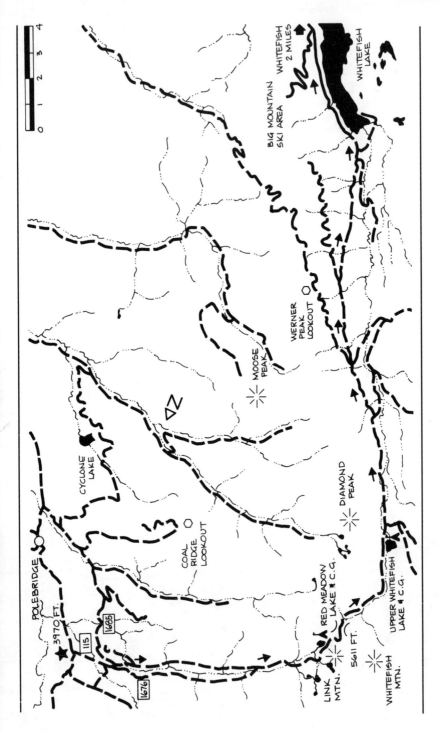

WHITEFISH LAKE

WHITEFISH 2 MILES

BIG MOUNTAIN SKI AREA

WERNER PEAK LOOKOUT

MOOSE PEAK

N

CYCLONE LAKE

COAL RIDGE LOOKOUT

DIAMOND PEAK

POLEBRIDGE

3970 FT.

115

1685

1676

RED MEADOW LAKE C.G.

LINK MTN.

5611 FT.

WHITEFISH MTN.

UPPER WHITEFISH LAKE C.G.

At 11.2 miles you arrive at the lake, which has a pleasant USFS campground on its shores. The climb steepens beyond the lake, but it's only about 9 miles to the Whitefish Divide, which you reach at 12.1. Near the divide you enter Stillwater State Forest, where the road quality deteriorates; it's a bumpy, steep downhill most of the way to Upper Whitefish Lake, at 16.8 miles. The campground here makes a nice lunch spot.

Now, if it's late July or early August, and as long as it hasn't been an unusually dry summer, you'll find yourself in huckleberry heaven! These delicious little cousins of the blueberry are one of the finest treats provided by Mother Nature. Browse around on the banks and upslope from the road, and you'll run into some good patches. Pick, eat, grin, and turn purple!

At 19.5 pass over a bridge, and at 22.0 miles turn left toward Whitefish. This turn is easy to miss, but *don't miss it*. Your ride once again roughens in here and becomes downright jolting at times. (If you have a shuttle driver, he should take the longer route into Whitefish unless he has four-wheel drive.) Keep your eyes open, for you'll be riding through some stands of giant white pine, a beautiful tree which is fairly uncommon in northwest Montana. Their size and straight grain make them a highly sought after lumber tree.

At a three-way junction at 24.2 miles, continue on the middle road; the left fork goes to Werner Peak Lookout. At 27.8 you ride by another road going left. At 32.8 bear left onto smooth gravel toward Whitefish, and at 33.7 you hit pavement. If you're allergic to riding on pavement, have your shuttle driver pick you up here. Or you can ride the remaining miles into downtown Whitefish, which you reach at 40.9 miles. Actually, the pavement should feel good after some of the rocks you've been riding over!

10

The Big Hole Valley and Pioneer Mountains

Within Montana, the Big Hole River Valley is known simply as the Big Hole. Although today it's one of the least populated sections of this sparsely peopled state (Beaverhead County, Montana's largest, covers 3,549,870 acres and contains fewer than 9000 residents), this southwestern Montana valley was actually among the earliest of areas in Montana to be settled. Lewis and Clark traveled just south of the Big Hole in 1805, and Captain Clark actually did pass through the Big Hole

Skeleton tepee frames, Big Hole Battlefield National Monument

Small, grassy meadows embraced by thick timber are common in the Pioneer Mountains.

in July 1806, on his way south to explore some of the country near present-day Yellowstone National Park. In 1862, Montana's first major gold strike took place on Grasshopper Creek at Bannack, just southeast of Big Hole Pass. This mining settlement subsequently became Montana's first territorial capital, and several thousand residents called it home. Bannack's heyday ended when gold production declined and the capital was moved to Virginia City, where the gold was rolling in. The ghost town of Bannack is now a state park, and well worth a visit.

What became the Big Hole's most infamous historical event took place at the eastern foot of Chief Joseph Pass, where today Montana State Highway 43 exits from the timber of the Bitterroot Range out into the irrigated basin. It was here, camped on an August morning in 1877, that Chief Joseph and his band of 800 displaced Nez Perce were attacked while sleeping by Colonel John Gibbon's U.S. troops and civilian volunteers. Big Hole Battlefield National Monument now stands where the Battle of the Big Hole took place. On the 600 acres of the monument, the National Park Service has established a visitor center and a haunting re-creation of the camping and battle grounds.

Today, the Big Hole is largely ranching country. Cattle spreads were first established in the mid-1800s, at the peak of the gold boom. It's also surrounded by timbered mountains. In a struggle to slow the clear-cutting of timber which has been escalating in recent years, Big Hole conservationists and lifelong ranchers have formed an alliance to try to change the USFS management policies in the surrounding Beaverhead National Forest.

Forming the western and southern rim of the Big Hole is the Bitterroot Range, along the crest of which runs the Continental Divide. The Pintlar Mountains close the northern end, and the Pioneer Mountains border the eastern side of the hole. Several commercial hot springs exist in the area, which make good base locations for mountain-biking rides. Just across the west side of the divide, about 20 miles northwest of Big Hole Battlefield National Monument, are two of Montana's nicest hot springs resorts; two somewhat more primitive ones lie on the east side of the divide.

A ride that looks promising on the Visitors Map is the Dry Creek Loop, which begins on Forest Road 934, a couple miles north of the Deep Creek Ski Area (which is 12 miles west and north of Wise River on State Highways 43 and 274).

The supplemental map for the Big Hole Valley and Pioneer Mountains is available from Beaverhead National Forest Supervisor's Office, 610 North Montana, Dillon, MT 59725, (406) 683-3900.

1 Historic Trail Loop

Riding surface:	smooth dirt or gravel to pavement
Beginning elevation:	6360 feet
Highest elevation:	7315 feet; 8034 feet for Anderson Mountain spur
Distance:	25.6 or 38.2 miles
Relative difficulty:	moderate
Time to allow:	3 to 8 hours
Best time of year:	June through October
Best time of week:	any day
Supplemental map:	Southwest Montana Interagency Visitors Map

A trusty steed rests along Historic Trail Loop.

Begin this ride at May Creek Campground (USFS), which is 9 miles east of Lost Trail Pass on Montana State Highway 43, or 17 miles west of Wisdom (often the coldest spot in the country!) on the same highway. Park at the campground and ride west on Hwy. 43, a portion of the TransAmerica Bicycle Trail. You'll crest Chief Joseph Pass and the Continental Divide on this wide, gently graded highway.

At 8.2 miles you have the option of turning left onto the Anderson Mountain Trail. The actual signing reads "Anderson Creek Trail 1.3, Cabinet Creek Trail 3.6, Anderson Mountain 6.5" (it's also signed with a "most difficult" ski-touring symbol). If you want to add this 12.6-mile round-trip onto your ride, see the description following the main ride narrative.

After 9.3 miles of pavement, immediately prior to the junction with US Highway 93 at Lost Trail Pass, turn right onto a road signed "Gibbons Pass /Hogan Cabin 5.5 miles." This road, which roughly follows the route that Colonel Gibbon used to approach the Nez Perce in the Big Hole, is signed as a ski-touring trail with a "more difficult" designation. Begin riding through a spruce and lodgepole pine forest. The road is smooth and gently uphill. Your riding here begins on the west side of the Continental Divide, actually in the Bitterroot National Forest. As you climb the ridge, you're afforded scenic views of Montana's Bitterroot Valley off to the left. You soon cross over to the east side of the divide back into the Beaverhead National Forest and remain there for the remainder of the ride.

At 10.6 note a road of slightly less quality going left; you continue right, uphill. At 10.8 you arrive at a high point and start down, and in another 0.1 mile continue bearing left on Gibbons Pass Road where Joseph Creek Road goes right.

At 12.0 miles you bottom out after a gentle downhill. The level road leads through an old clear-cut which contains much new growth. At 12.9 another downhill takes you into the burn of 1985. At 13.8, still in the burn, you arrive at a junction. A blue ski sign points to the right, which is a shortcut to Hogan Cabin (taking this road would save about 4 miles). Continue straight, leaving the burn and riding back into spruce forest for a short ways before re-entering the burn at 14.1 miles.

At 15.3 you bottom out after a gentle downhill, and at 16.0 you arrive at a T. Turn sharp right, and cross the bridge over Trail Creek; begin following the creek downstream. This road, a stretch of the Lewis and Clark Historical Trail, is somewhat more primitive than the one you just turned off of. At 16.8 you once again enter the large burn. At 17.8 miles, Forest Road 1269/Prairie Creek Road climbs to the left; you bear right, staying low. At 18.2 cross a cattle guard and enter a large meadow in 0.2 mile. At 18.6 is the road which goes to Hogan Cabin, which you can see on your right; continue straight unless you want to go in and have a closer look at the cabin. The shortcut road mentioned at mile 13.8 comes in immediately in front of this USFS cabin.

At 19.6 Sunshine Creek comes in on your right. This stretch of road is particularly enticing as it meanders on the level through wildflower-studded meadows. At 22.1 miles the Elk Creek/Continental Divide Trail takes off to the left. At 24.0, turn left back onto Hwy. 43 (the road you're turning off of is signed, at this point, "Bitterroot/Big Hole Road Snow Trail"). After 1.6 miles on the pavement, you return to May Creek Campground at 25.6 miles.

Oh, that water's cold!

If you'd like to tack on the Anderson Mountain ride, which is recommended if time and energy permit, back at 8.2 miles turn left, and begin some serious roller-coaster riding through a thick forest canopy. At 0.6 mile bear straight ahead rather than heading off on a road to the right. At 1.3 you pass a ski-touring sign which reads "Richardson Creek Trail/

US Hwy. 43 2 miles" (to the left). At 2.4 miles you enter an open meadow which offers big views into Idaho.

At 3.2 you hit a steep, rocky uphill. At 4.4 continue following the blue ski diamonds, as a lesser-quality road takes off to the left. At 5.3 miles another road departs to the left; you go straight up a big hill and switchback to the right at 5.5 miles. You continue straight ahead; the road becomes rocky, but levels out. At 6.3 miles you arrive at the former site of the Anderson Mountain Lookout. Although the lookout is gone, the cement foundation blocks remain — and the views are still there! The elevation here is 8034 feet. You've gained just under 800 feet since leaving the highway. Turn around and retrace your tracks; when you get back to the highway, turn left and pick up the Historic Trail Loop narrative at mile 8.2.

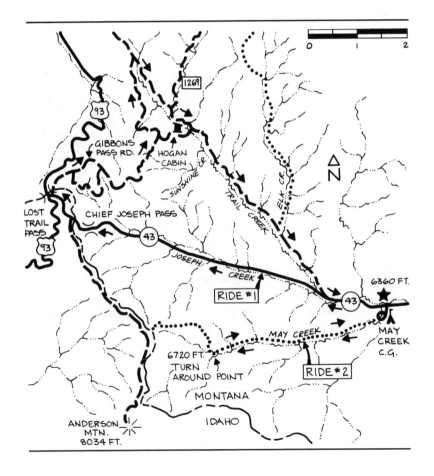

2 May Creek Out and Back

Riding surface:	mostly smooth dirt trail with some rocks and roots
Beginning elevation:	6360 feet
Highest elevation:	6720 feet
Distance:	10 miles
Relative difficulty:	easy
Time to allow:	2 to 3 hours
Best time of year:	June through October
Best time of week:	weekdays during summer; any day during fall
Supplemental map:	Southwest Montana Interagency Visitors Map

This is a short, enjoyable trail ride, perfect for an early morning "wildlife pedal" or as an after-supper digestion-helper. The trail begins near Site 13 at the May Creek Campground, the same campground where Ride 1 begins. Pass through the gate behind the campsite (close the gate behind you), and follow the trail straight across the small meadow. At 0.1 mile walk your bike over to the right side of May Creek on a two-log bridge. If you look into the deep hole below and to the right of the logs, you're liable to see a number of pan-sized brook trout. The trail continues along the north side of the creek through meadow and occasionally through forest of lodgepole pine and Douglas fir. At 1.9 miles you see, to your right, the first in a series of old cabins. These were associated with early placer mining along the creek. You then come out of the forest back into a large meadow, where willows line the stream.

At 2.3 miles note another cabin off to the left across the creek, and at 2.6 cross a drainage that will likely be chopped up by cattle's hooves. At 3.8 you get up onto a rocky sidehill; this doesn't last for long, however. At 4.0 the trail becomes very smooth as it once again enters the woods. At 4.3 miles you cross a small feeder stream, and at 4.5, after you crest a small hill, there's another old cabin. At 4.8 you ride by yet another cabin, this one virtually *on* the trail. At about 5.0 even, where two creeks merge to form May Creek, the trail becomes more indistinct and begins climbing sharply to the right. This is the end of the easy riding; turn around here.

3 Saginaw Mountain Loop

Riding surface:	rough gravel to smooth dirt
Beginning elevation:	7020 feet
Highest elevation:	7970 feet
Distance:	20.1 miles
Relative difficulty:	moderate
Time to allow:	3 to 5 hours
Best time of year:	June through Oct 15; road closed seasonally after October 15 to protect wildlife
Best time of week:	any day
Supplemental map:	Southwest Montana Interagency Visitors Map

Near the top of the hill 0.5 mile south of the classic western town of Jackson, on State Highway 278, turn right onto Bloody Dick Road. Proceed to South Van Houten Campground, or nearby North Van Houten Campground, both of which are 11 miles from Hwy. 278. Generally, this ride can be described as one which crosses over from drainage to drainage, resulting in relatively short uphills and downhills: in other words, a roller coaster. Although the scenery is not spectacular and you pass many clear-cuts which you may consider ugly, the fun factor on this ride is very high!

Leave South Van Houten Campground and turn left. At 0.5 bear right at the Y (bearing left would lead you to North Van Houten Campground). You're riding along the sage-covered bench above the upper reaches of the Big Hole River. At 2.0 miles turn right toward Saginaw Mountain. At 2.1 miles cross the river, then a cattle guard, and start uphill on a rugged, bumpy surface. You're still riding amidst the pungent sage, but timber is closing in on the sides. At the Y at 2.6, go right and begin a gentle uphill. At 3.0 another road veers left; you continue bearing right uphill. At 3.3 cross a cattle guard, and at 3.8 top out at a high point and bear right.

At 4.2 miles break out into an opening which offers a good view of the Bitterroot Range on the right. This road can be quite dusty if you ride it during a dry spell. You ride past many small, relatively new clear-cuts. Note that most of them took place in stands of spindly lodgepoles. The USFS hopes that opening up some of these dense forests will stimulate the growth of elk food supplies.

At 4.8 miles begin another uphill. Note that as you gain elevation you encounter more Douglas fir. At 5.3 miles top out; begin a short downhill in another 0.1 mile. At 5.8 you curve right across the drainage

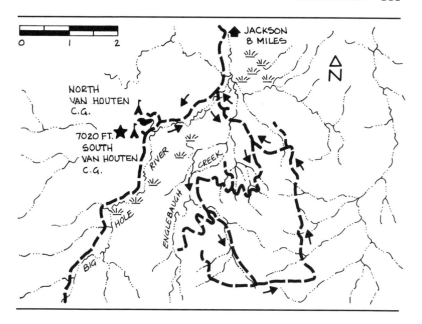

bottom and begin up. At 6.0 the road levels off, then starts down. At 6.8 you pass by a gated road on your right. At 7.1 miles cross over to the other side of the drainage and begin up. At 7.7 you top out on a saddle and start down the other side. Initially, the riding is along a ledge, with good views to the right. At 8.3 you bottom out and start up once again, crossing the East Fork of Englebaugh Creek and turning sharp left to parallel it upstream along an unsigned, lesser-quality road (the road surface you're turning off of continues to the right). This becomes a narrow double-track which winds through a thick forest canopy.

At 8.8 miles ride through the stream and continue upstream along its left side on this fun forest path. At 10.3 you bisect a small meadow and at 10.6, at the top of a ridge and a clear-cut, turn left at the T onto a well-graded road. At 10.9 pass through a gate and over a cattle guard, and then begin a downhill. During the next 2 miles, you pass by a series of roads which are closed permanently for habitat recovery. The road on which you're riding has many drainage dips built into it; some are fun stomach-risers while others are potentially hazardous, so be on the lookout.

At 12.4 miles bottom out at a drainage and start a gentle uphill. At 13.0 again cross a drainage and continue up, and at 13.5 miles begin a gentle downhill. At 14.0 you pass through a gate (which, like several others you've ridden through, will be locked shut after October 15) and start a gradual uphill. At 14.4 cross a cattle guard and begin down, and at 15.2 switchback hard left and continue down (another road bears up to the right). At 16.1 you hit bottom and begin up.

At the Y at 16.3 continue straight, heading down. At 16.8 cross a cattle guard, and at 18.0 cross another cattle guard back out into the willow bottoms. At 18.1 turn left at the junction, and return to South Van Houten Campground, at 20.1 miles.

4 Bryant–Calvert Hill Loop

Riding surface:	smooth dirt to very bumpy talus
Beginning elevation:	5725 feet
Highest elevation:	7618 feet
Distance:	18.8 miles
Relative difficulty:	hard
Time to allow:	3 to 5 hours
Best time of year:	June through October
Best time of week:	any day
Supplemental map:	Southwest Montana Interagency Visitors Map

This ride is called the Bryant–Calvert *Hill* Loop because, really, there is only one hill in the ride— and it's the entire ride! Up 6.5 miles and 8.3 miles down, plus some roller-coaster riding along the river.

From State Highway 43, at 7 miles west of the settlement of Wise River, turn south onto Bryant Creek Road. You cross the Big Hole River

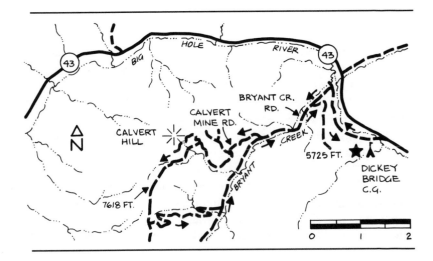

on Dickey Bridge and arrive at a BLM campground where you can park. Begin riding west on Bryant Creek Rd., which parallels the river for a couple of miles. At 2.0 miles, follow the road as it curves left, away from the river. It narrows at this point and begins to head gradually uphill as you parallel Bryant Creek.

At 3.1 you continue bearing right up Bryant Creek (left goes to Teddy Creek). At 3.7 cross over to the right side of the creek and begin riding on extremely bumpy, angular rock at the foot of a long talus slope. At 4.4 miles bear right uphill at the Y onto Calvert Mine Road. The surface becomes smooth dirt, and the grade steepens drastically at this point. Gear down for a long uphill. You'll be passing through a series of clear-cuts along the way.

At 5.6 miles note a closed road off to your right. At 6.1 continue up to the right. At 6.4 you cross a cattle guard and come into a large mining and quarry area. At 6.7 a lesser-quality road goes right; continue following the similar surface to the left. At several of the junctions, you'll note directional arrows pointing the way you want to go with the words "Forest Service Designated Route" printed on the sign.

At 7.7 miles continue right (uphill) through an old clear-cut. Most of this ride takes place in steep, protected drainages, so the views you have to your right here should be cherished. At 8.5 miles you finally top out at a cattle guard after 4 steep miles. At this point you start back down into the Bryant Creek drainage on a smooth, double-track road. This is a huge, heavily timbered drainage. As you head down you pass through more undisturbed timber stands than you did going up. At 8.8 miles you pass a big rock point on your left. At 9.5 bear left at the fork.

At 10.1 miles curve hard left. At 11.7 switchback left, then at 12.0 switchback right across the drainage bottom. At 12.7 miles merge left onto the Bryant Creek Rd. (you'd have to turn sharp right to go the wrong way), heading downstream. At 12.8 you cross a cattle guard, and at 14.6 you close the loop and once again ride across the bumpy talus. At 16.7 leave the Beaverhead National Forest and curve right to once again parallel the Big Hole River. At 18.8 you're back at your point of origin.

Appendices

A. More Rides in the Northern Rockies

Time and space limit the number of areas that could be covered in this guide, but you can order the Visitors Map for any national forest in the Northern Rockies and discover for yourself a wealth of riding opportunities in each. Though you have to be a bit more selective in order to find aesthetically pleasing riding on BLM lands, there are plenty of good places to ride on lands administered by that agency, as well. For good measure, here are a few more favorite spots for riding in the Northern Rockies and how to go about getting the maps for them.

MONTANA

The Rocky Mountain Front

Some of the best and most seldom-viewed scenery in Montana is along the east front of the Rockies, roughly from the town of Browning on the north to just south of Augusta, which is 50 miles west of Great Falls and 75 miles north of Helena. This is where the mountains meet the

The Sun River Wildlife Management Area, along Montana's Rocky Mountain Front, offers miles of fun mountain-biking roads.

Pishkun Canal Road, along Montana's Rocky Mountain Front

plains, which seem to extend endlessly to the east. A large share of the northern part, bordering on Glacier National Park, is Blackfeet tribal lands. The best riding opportunities are on lands administered by the Lewis and Clark National Forest and the Montana Department of Fish, Wildlife and Parks.

One of the best rides *anywhere* is on the Sun River Wildlife Management Area, 12 miles northwest of the town of Augusta. This is rolling, pine-studded country — not yet mountains, and yet not plains, but a delightful combination of the two. So perfectly suited is the terrain here for mountain biking that, if it were within 50 miles of Los Angeles, they'd have to erect stop signs and traffic lights in order to control all the bicycle traffic! But it's nowhere near L.A., and you won't be likely to encounter other cyclists, or even cars. It's important grizzly habitat and elk wintering grounds, and the miles of roads within are closed to traffic between December 1 and May 15. For further details, contact the Department of Fish, Wildlife, and Parks in Great Falls, at (406) 454-3441.

Two other good rides begin at Home Gulch Campground (USFS), which is near the mouth of the Sun River Canyon, approximately 20 miles northwest of Augusta. One follows an old road which parallels Pishkun Canal 19 miles out onto the plains; the other parallels the Sun River upstream for a couple of miles before going south on Forest Road 233/ Beaver Creek Road, in front of some huge, dramatically folded mountain walls.

The map for this area is the Lewis and Clark National Forest Visitors Map (Rocky Mountain Division), available from Forest Supervisor's Office; P.O. Box 871; Great Falls, MT 59403; phone (406) 791-7700.

The Yaak

Occupying the extreme northwest corner of Montana are the Purcell Mountains, which are drained by the Kootenai River, in part via the Yaak River. The area is quite similar to the North Fork (Chapter 9) in its remoteness and thick forest cover. Miles and miles of roads which have been closed to four-wheel traffic are available to the mountain biker.

Two suggested rides would lead you to the Northwest Peak Scenic Area, and to Grubstake Mountain. The map you need for the Yaak is the Kootenai National Forest Visitors Map, available from Forest Supervisor's Office; RR 3, Box 700; Libby. MT 59923; phone (406) 293-6211.

Missouri Breaks

Out in the big, big open spaces of northeastern Montana, fascinating landforms have been carved by the Missouri River waters. Charles M. Russell National Wildlife Refuge and U.L. Bend National Wildlife Refuge both contain many miles of roads which would provide good mountain biking. This is a part of the 15,000-square-mile section of the state proposed by Missoula's Institute of the Rockies to be reverted to wild grazing lands for native animals and called The Big Open.

You can obtain the maps for the Missouri Breaks and adjacent country by contacting Lewistown District BLM; Airport Road; Lewistown, MT 59457; phone (406) 538-7461.

Crazy Mountains

The Crazies are a small, isolated range just northeast of Livingston, which is 50 miles north of Yellowstone National Park. They are administered in part by the Gallatin National Forest and partly by the Lewis and Clark National Forest. Information on where to obtain these maps is in Chapter 3 and above, under "The Rocky Mountain Front." The northern half of the Crazies are laced with jeep and logging roads ideal for mountain biking.

Pryor Mountain Wild Horse Range

North of Wyoming's Bighorn Mountains (Chapter 2), 60 miles south of Billings, lives a herd of about 150 wild horses which some say are the closest thing left in this country to the pure mustangs the Spanish conquistadors brought to the New World in the 1500s.

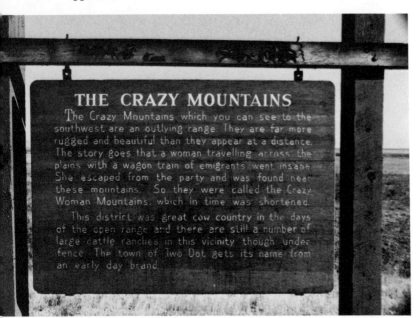

How the Crazy Mountains got their name

This sage-covered country above the Bighorn Canyon was declared the first federal wild horse range in the United States in 1968. There is some good exploring by mountain bike to be done here, and opportunities abound for seeing wildlife other than the horses. Maps are available through Billings BLM Resource Area; 810 E. Main St.; Billings, MT 59101; phone (406) 657-6262.

IDAHO

Salmon

The areas west and east of the town of Salmon, 140 miles south of Missoula, Montana, offer superb riding potential. A good multi-day loop could be accomplished by heading east, over into the Big Hole (Chapter 10), and back over the Bitterroots once again to Salmon. To the west is a heavily forested mountainous area which contains a plethora of logging roads. There are some undeveloped hot springs in this area which you can seek out to soak in. Obtain the Salmon National Forest Visitors Map from Forest Supervisor's Office; P.O. Box 729; Salmon, ID 83467; phone (208) 756-2215.

Big Hole Mountains

On the west side of Teton Pass, just across the mountains from Jackson Hole in Wyoming, are the Big Hole Mountains (not to be confused with The Big Hole Valley, which is covered in Chapter 10). This rolling, not overtly spectacular range is largely bypassed by visitors to the area. But local ski tourists have discovered some of the best terrain for their activity lies here. And mountain bikers, likewise, are finding the rolling land perfect for their pursuit. To gain access to these mountains, you can take State Highway 31 a few miles southwest from the town of Victor, or head due west from Driggs on the only paved road leading that direction from town. The range is depicted on the Targhee National Forest Visitors Map. Ordering information for this map is in Chapter 3.

Clearwater River Drainage

The Clearwater River drainage is a huge triangle of thickly forested mountains defined roughly by Interstate 90 from Missoula, Montana, to Kellogg, Idaho; US Highway 12 from Missoula to Kooskia, Idaho; and closed on the west by an imaginary north-south line running from Kellogg to Kooskia. Very few people live within this triangle, and it contains hundreds of miles of logging roads. The land within it is administered primarily by the Clearwater National Forest Supervisor's Office; Route 1; Orofino, ID 83544; phone (208) 476-4541 and the St. Joe National Forest Supervisor's Office; 1201 Ironwood Drive; Coeur d'Alene, ID 83814; phone (208) 765-7223.

The best access into the heart of this country is the road — mostly gravel — which runs between Superior, Montana, and Orofino, Idaho. If you study an Idaho state map, this triangle will become obvious.

Boise and Challis National Forests

Both of these forests, which lie in southwestern to southcentral Idaho, contain hundreds of miles of logging roads. Maps indicate that they contain potential for a great many long, multi-day tours (more so than some of the other forests in the region). Mountain bikes are becoming a common sight along these forests' gravel and dirt pathways.

The Visitors Maps are available from Boise National Forest Supervisor's Office; 1750 Front St.; Boise, ID 83702; phone (208) 334-1516 and Challis National Forest Supervisor's Office; Challis, ID 83226; phone (208) 879-2285.

NORTHERN WYOMING

Union Pass Area

From the north end of Wyoming State Highway 352 (the Green River Lakes Road, which departs from US Highway 191 just west of the town of Pinedale, in west central Wyoming), the primitive Tepee Creek Road will lead you into some fascinating country. There is a wealth of roads off Pinyon Ridge and in the Union Pass vicinity. You can ultimately pick your way out to US Highway 287 and to the town of Dubois. In doing this you would pass through a narrow corridor which separates the Jim Bridger and Gros Ventre wilderness areas. Some of these roads are within the Shoshone National Forest, but nearly the entire area is depicted on the Bridger-Teton National Forest maps. Ordering information for the Bridger-Teton maps is in Chapter 4.

Owl Creek and Bridger Mountains

The which? Not many people have heard of these mountains near Thermopolis, in north-central Wyoming. This is actually a single range which is split down the middle by the Wind River Canyon (north of the canyon the Wind becomes the Big Horn River, by the way). This low range extends from the southern end of the Bighorn Mountains westward to near the town of Dubois. The part east of the Wind River Canyon is known as the Bridger Mountains; that west is called the Owl Creeks. For information and maps for this area, contact the Worland BLM Resource District; Worland, WY 82401; phone (307) 347-9871.

Mountains of the Wyoming-Idaho Border

These are long, linear mountain ridges along the Overthrust Belt, an area famous among geologists and oil companies for the fossil fuels contained within. From northeast to southwest the ranges are the Hobacks, the Wyomings, and the Salt Rivers. The latter two are separated by the valley of the Grey's River, which empties into the Snake River southwest of Hoback Junction. These mountains are largely uninhabited and little visited, except by a few sportsmen and the people involved with ongoing fossil-fuel exploration and development. They contain some glorious creeks and peaks and roads for mountain biking. They are primarily within the Bridger-Teton National Forest, Bridger West Division. You can obtain the necessary maps through the Bridger-Teton National Forest Supervisor's Office, the information for which is detailed in Chapter 4.

Crossing a stream en route to the Union Pass area (Wyoming)

NORTH DAKOTA

The Badlands

Just across the border from Montana, south of Watford City, North Dakota, and north of the town of Medora, are the two units of Theodore Roosevelt National Park. There, and in the lands surrounding the park, the Little Missouri River and its feeder streams have eroded the prairie into a ghostly wonderland. Roads within and outside of the park offer riding through this unique area. Eroded, sculptured figures seem to come alive in the first and last light of day. For information on the area, contact Theodore Roosevelt National Park; Medora, ND 58645; phone (701) 623-4466.

Other Northern Rockies National Forests

Here is a listing of other national forests within the region, along with their addresses. You can order maps directly from them.

Coeur d'Alene National Forest; 1201 Ironwood Dr.; Coeur d'Alene, ID 83814; phone (208) 765-7561.

Nezperce National Forest; Route 2, Box 475; Grangeville, ID 83530; phone (208) 983-1950.

Caribou National Forest; Federal Building, Suite 294; Pocatello, ID 83201; phone (208) 236-6700. The Caribou National Forest USFS Travel Plan Map specifically addresses bicycles along with other ORVs.

Ground squirrel is tempted by a camp treat.

Bitterroot National Forest; 316 N. 3rd St.; Hamilton, MT 59840; phone
(406) 363-3131.
Deerlodge National Forest; P.O. Box 400, Federal Building; Butte, MT
59701; phone (406) 723-6561.
Helena National Forest; Federal Building, Drawer 10014; Helena, MT
59626; phone (406) 449-5201.

B. Recommended Reading

MOUNTAIN BIKING

All-Terrain Bikes, the editors of *Bicycling* magazine. Rodale Press, 1985.

The Cyclists' Yellow Pages, Bikecentennial Publications, 1988. A resource guide for the cycle-tourist, which includes a general listing of places to ride mountain bikes throughout the United States and Canada.

Eugene Sloane's Complete Book of All-Terrain Bicycles, Eugene A. Sloane. Simon & Schuster, 1985.

The Mountain Bike Adventure Guide for the Sun Valley Area, John Zilly and Eloise Christensen. John Zilly, 1987.

The Mountain Bike Book, Rob Van der Plas. Bicycle Books, Inc., 1984.

Mountain Bike Manual, Dennis Coello. Dream Garden Press, 1985.

A Mountain Biker's Guide to the Black Hills of South Dakota and Wyoming, D. Horning and H. Marriott. Poorperson's Guidebooks, 1987.

GENERAL BICYCLING

Anybody's Bike Book, Tom Cuthbertson. Ten Speed Press, 1984. A guide to maintenance and repair.

The Bike Bag Book, Tom Cuthbertson. Ten Speed Press, 1981. A good one to carry along while riding, in case of mechanical problems.

Complete Guide to Bicycle Maintenance and Repair, the editors of *Bicycling* magazine. Rodale Press, 1986.

Freewheeling: Bicycling the Open Road, Gary Ferguson. The Mountaineers, 1984. Good general information, much of which can be adapted to mountain biking.

Glenn's Complete Bicycle Manual, Clarence W. Coles and Harold T. Glenn. Crown Publishers, 1987. A guide to maintenance and repair.

Richard's Bicycle Book, Richard Ballantine. Random House, 1982. A guide to maintenance and repair.

Roadside Bicycle Repairs, Rob Van der Plas. Bicycle Books, Inc., 1987.

FIRST AID

Mountaineering First Aid, The Mountaineers, 1975.

Mountaineering Medicine, Fred T. Darvill, M.D. Wilderness Press, 1983.

Standard First Aid and Personal Safety, the American Red Cross. Doubleday & Company, 1979.

MOUNTAINEERING AND CAMPING

Be an Expert with Map and Compass, Bjorn Kjellstrom. Scribner, 1976.
Mountaineering — The Freedom of the Hills. The Mountaineers, 1982.
Largely concerned with climbing, this book contains basics every outdoors recreationist should be familiar with.
Rand McNally RV Park and Campground Directory: United States, Canada, and Mexico. Rand McNally & Company, 1988. Information-packed directory which includes listings of both private and public campgrounds.

FLORA AND FAUNA

Guide to the Natural Areas of Idaho, Montana, and Wyoming, John Perry and Jane Greverus Perry. Sierra Club Books, 1988.
Mammals, William H. Burt and Richard P. Grossenheider. Houghton Mifflin Company, 1976.
Rocky Mountain Wildflowers, Ron Taylor. The Mountaineers, 1986.
Rocky Mountain Wildflowers, Craighead, Craighead, and Davis. Houghton Mifflin Company, 1963.
Western Birds, Roger Tory Peterson. Houghton Mifflin Company, 1961.
Western Forests, Stephen Whitney. Alfred A. Knopf, 1985.

GEOLOGY

Geology of the Black Hills, F. J. Rich. American Geological Institute, 1981.
Guidebook to the Geology of Northern and Western Idaho and Surrounding Areas, Roy Breckenridge. Idaho Geological Survey, 1988.
Guidebook to the Geology of Southern and Central Idaho, Carl Link. Idaho Geological Survey, 1987.
Pages of Stone: Geology of Western National Parks and Monuments, Volume 1, Halka Chronic. The Mountaineers, 1984.
Roadside Geology of Montana, David Alt and Donald W. Hyndman. Mountain Press Publishing Company, 1986.
Roadside Geology of the Yellowstone Country, William J. Fritz. Mountain Press Publishing Company, 1985.
Traveler's Guide to the Geology of Wyoming, D. L. Blackstone. Geological Survey of Wyoming, 1982.

DIET AND COOKBOOKS

Cycle Food: A Guide to Satisfying Your Inner Tube, Lauren Hefferon. Ten Speed Press, 1983.

NOLS Cookery, the National Outdoor Leadership School. Emporia State Press, 1980.

C. Additional Map and Information Sources

Distribution Branch, U.S. Geological Survey; Box 25286, Federal Center Bldg. 41; Denver, CO 80225; phone (303) 236-7477. Contact for a key to all the U.S. Geological Survey topographic maps.

Bureau of Land Management; Department of the Interior; Office of Public Affairs; 18th & C St., NW; Washington, DC 20240; phone (202) 343-5717. Contact for maps covering lands administered by the BLM.

Superintendent of Documents; U.S. Government Printing Office; Washington, DC 20402. Contact for a map and key to all lands administered by the National Park Service.

Idaho Travel Council; Statehouse; Boise, ID 83720; phone (800) 635-7820 (out-of-state) or (208) 334-2470 (in-state).

Travel Montana; 1424 9th Ave.; Helena, MT 59620; phone (800) 548-3390 (out-of-state) or (406) 444-2654 (in-state).

North Dakota Tourism Promotion Division; State Capitol Grounds; Bismarck, ND 58505; phone (800) 437-2077 (out-of-state) or (701) 472-2100 (in-state).

South Dakota Tourism Development; 711 Wells; Pierre, SD 57501; phone (800) 843-1930 (out-of-state) or (800) 952-2217 (in-state).

Wyoming Travel Commission; I-25 at College Drive; Cheyenne, WY 82002; phone (800) 225-5996 (out-of-state) or (307) 777-7777 (in-state).

Bikecentennial; P.O. Box 8308; Missoula, MT 59801; phone (406) 721-1776.

D. Mail-Order Equipment

Bikecology, 1515 Wilshire, Santa Monica, CA 90403.

Bike Nashbar, 4111 Simon, Youngstown, OH 44512.

Campmoor, P.O. Box 998, Paramus, NJ 07653.

Cycle Goods, 2735 Hennepin Ave. S., Minneapolis, MN 55408.

Eastern Mountain Sports, Vose Farm Rd., Peterborough, NH 03458.

Eddie Bauer, Box 3700, Seattle, WA 98124.

L.L. Bean, Freeport, ME 04032.

Recreational Equipment, Inc., P.O. Box C-88125, Seattle, WA 98188-0125.

Index

About the author:

When Michael McCoy was nine years old, he was foolishly riding his old two-speed Schwinn down a residential street while reading the latest issued of MAD magaine.

"Suddenly I sensed a tremendous reduction in my forward momentum, and found myself sprawled atop the rear end of a parked Pontiac. I had pedalled straight into the behemoth!" he recalls. It was then he first suspected that he wasn't cut out to bicycle on pavement, with cars and trucks. Many years later he first tried mountain biking, and he took to it at once.

After graduating from the University of Wyoming in 1973 with a degree in anthropology, McCoy performed "contract" archaeology for Western Wyoming College for several summers. He also spent time as a park ranger at Devils Tower National Monument and as a wildlife technician for the Kootenai National Forest.

McCoy joined the staff of Bikecentennial, the "Bicycle Travel Association," in 1976, and has had a hand in developing their 16,000-mile National Bicycle Trails Network. He is now their program director, and a contributing editor of *Bike Report*.

In this guide he combines his skill as a bicycle route finder with his love for the mountains and their resident wildlife. He is active in many different "self-propelled" activities, from marathon running to backpacking to cross-country skiing to mountain biking. McCoy and his wife, Nancy, have bicycled (both on- and off-pavement) throughout the United States.

"I love the sensation of motion," says McCoy. "Moving through the countryside — rather than arriving at a destination — is always my primary 'goal'."

The McCoys reside in Missoula, Montana.